Dennis Mahoney
c/o 815 Wash ave.
Detroit Lakes, Minn.

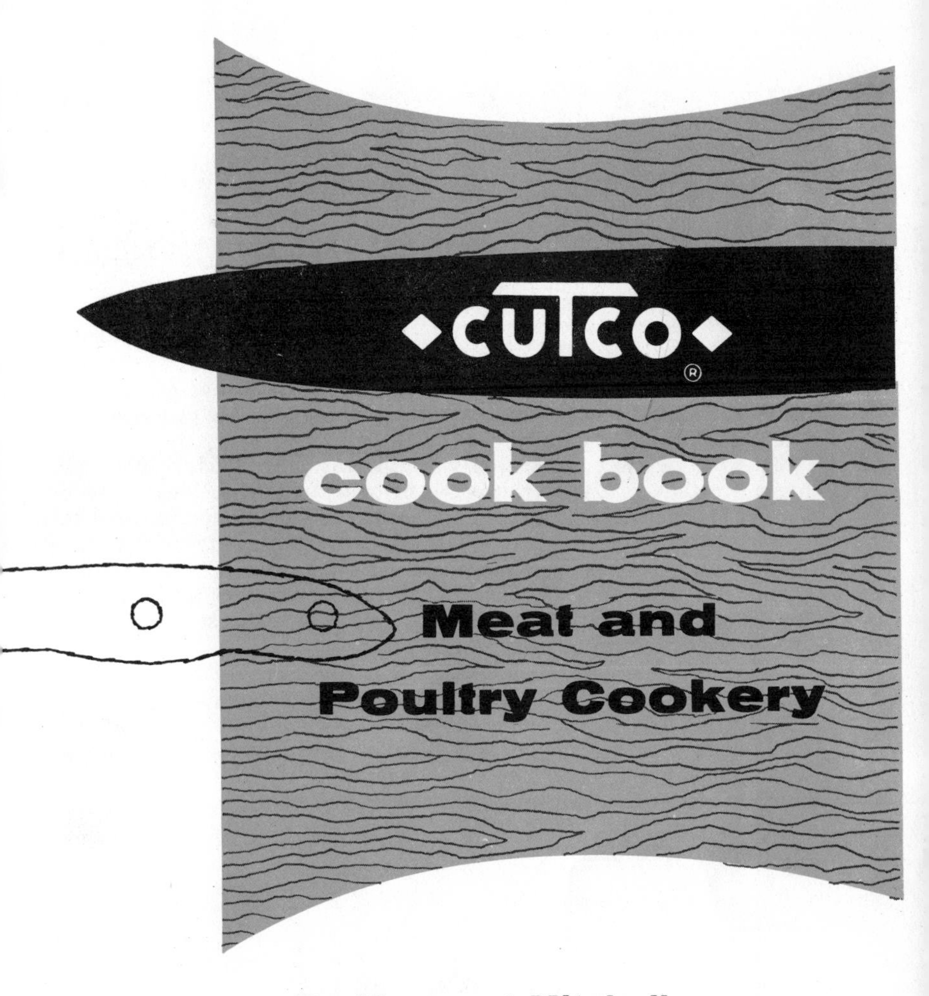

By Margaret Mitchell
Director, Home Economics

VOLUME ONE

Line illustrations by Frank Marcello

Published by CUTCO DIVISION

Meat Is Important

Down through the centuries meat has always been one of the most universally liked foods. It is the heart of the meal—the center around which the menu is planned.

There is pleasure associated with the eating of foods which have appeal to the eye and to the senses of taste and smell. Meat presents a mouth watering picture and its aroma and flavor tempt even the most jaded appetite.

The belief of some that meat is not as digestible as other foods is erroneous. Meat may take longer to digest than other foods but this is one of the points in its favor, for this slower digestion gives you that satisfied feeling at the end of a meal.

Aside from its great palatability it is necessary to the daily diet because it is such a rich source of the highest quality protein. It also furnishes valuable amounts of health guarding vitamins and minerals such as iron, copper and phosphorus which go into the making of good blood and bones. Even the fat on meat is of high energy value.

Meat can always be fitted into the budget because the less tender cuts which are the least expensive are just as nutritious as the more expensive tender cuts.

NEED FOR VARIETY

If the family sits down to the table, takes one look and says "I'm not hungry" the reason is almost always a lack of appetite appeal either in the food itself or in its preparation.

It is true menus should be planned to give the necessary daily food requirements, but it is of equal importance that there is variety. Frequent repetition of foods or combinations of foods or repetition of the same foods at regular intervals make meals monotonous.

No article of diet lends itself more readily to variety in menu making than does meat. First of all, there are the various kinds of meat in many different cuts from which to choose—beef, veal, pork, lamb, turkey, chicken and duck, all of which are available the year around.

In addition to the kinds and cuts of meats, there are hundreds of different methods of preparing and cooking each. Get out of the rut you are in—try different cuts, prepare them in different ways and serve a different kind of meat each day.

Then the "I'm not hungry" will be replaced with "when do we eat" —real music to the ears of every good cook.

GUIDES TO MEAT BUYING

Since a large part of the weekly food budget is spent for meat, one should know how to select good meat as well as prepare it properly.

Basically, there are three guides to follow in buying meat. They are (1) the inspection stamp (2) the grade stamp and (3) the appearance of the meat itself.

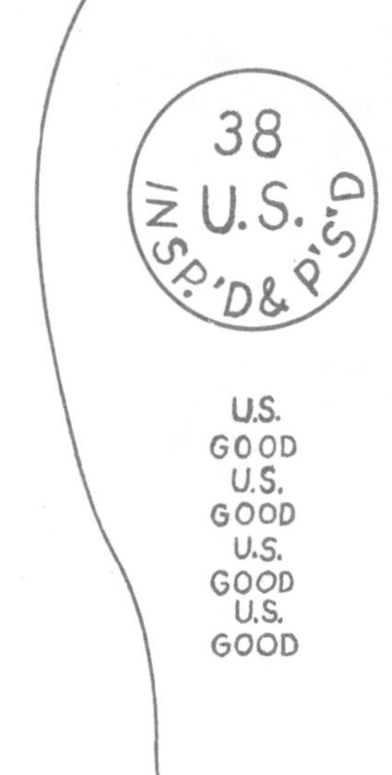

The Inspection Stamp is a round purple stamp used to indicate the meat has passed federal, state or city inspection. It is your assurance that the meat is wholesome. The marking fluid used for this stamp is a vegetable coloring and is harmless. It need not be trimmed from the meat.

The Grade Stamp runs like a purple ribbon the length of the carcass and designates the quality of the meat. The official U. S. grades—prime, choice, good, commercial and utility are the ones found at most meat counters. Many packers also use special brand names to designate various qualities. If the packer is well-known his grades could be considered reliable—otherwise it is safer to look for the U. S. grades.

As to appearance, the meat should be bright in color, moist and free of odor. The fat should be creamy white and firm. In the case of quality beef, there should be abundant marbling (thin lines of fat through the meat).

U. S. GRADE STAMPS FOR BEEF, VEAL, LAMB, MUTTON

U. S. Prime—This is the highest grade. The supply is limited and very little is available in retail markets.

U. S. Choice—This stamp usually indicates the highest grade found in retail markets. Such meat is well marbled with fat and has a moderately thick covering of fat.

U. S. Good—This stamp indicates the highest grade of meat sold in volume throughout the year. The fat covering is usually slightly thinner and the marbling less extensive.

U. S. Commercial—U. S. Utility—These stamps indicate lower grades. The fat covering is thin and there is little or no marbling. These grades are cheaper and best suited for braising or pot roasting.

CARE OF MEAT IN THE HOME

The meat you buy should be properly cared for to insure its freshness.

Steaks, chops and **roasts** have considerable surface exposed to air and therefore, will not keep too long. Remove wrapping paper as soon as possible. Scrape or wipe off any visible dirt or slivers of bone. Do not wash. Cover lightly with Alcoa Wrap leaving ends open. Store in coldest part of refrigerator or in meat compartment. These cuts should not be kept more than two or three days.

Ground meats should be handled the same as steaks and chops. Cook within 24 hours since chopped meats are more perishable. If it is necessary to keep them a greater length of time, they should be shaped into cooking portions and frozen.

Smoked meats with a mild cure such as hams and bacon need the same attention as fresh meats. Store in the coldest part of the refrigerator to retain their fresh flavor; do not hold longer than two weeks.

Variety meats such as liver, kidneys, hearts and sweetbreads should be cooked within 24 hours. Otherwise, they should be frozen.

Cooked meats should always be kept in the refrigerator. They should be covered or wrapped in Alcoa Wrap and stored in the refrigerator as soon as the meal is over. It is not necessary they be cooled first.

Temporary freezing is helpful when it is necessary to keep meat more than two or three days. It should be tightly wrapped in Alcoa Wrap and stored in the freezer compartment. Once it has been thawed it should never be refrozen but should be used at once.

• CUTCO •

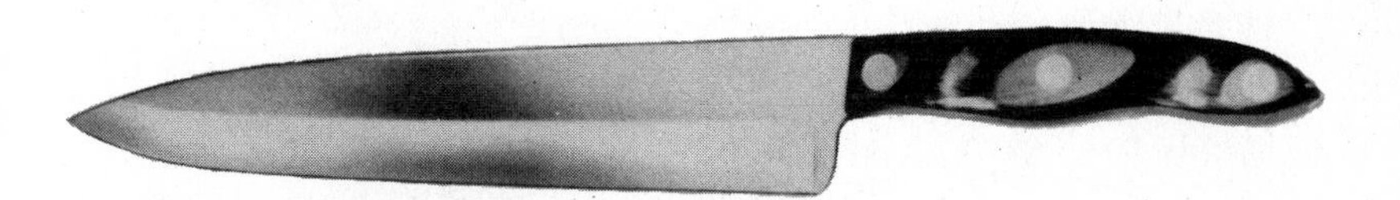

French Chef's Knife

Directions for Use:

1. Place food to be chopped on chopping board.

2. Grasp handle of French Chef's Knife between thumb and forefinger of right hand with fingers following curve of handle.

3. Place tip of blade on cutting board at a 45 degree angle with surface of board.

4. Place thumb and fingers of left hand on tip of blade, holding it firmly to the board.

5. Move knife down and up in a rocking motion keeping tip of blade on the board; at the same time move knife back and forth across board in a quarter circle.

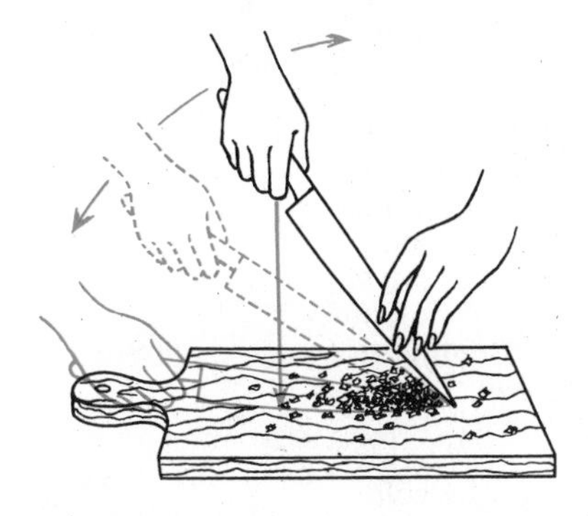

Note:

1. When dicing celery, carrots, green beans, etc., place 8-10 pieces lengthwise on chopping board.

2. Hold pieces firmly with left hand.

3. Slowly push pieces under blade of French Chef's Knife; at same time move knife down and up in rocking motion.

Uses:

- Chopping greens (cabbage, celery, lettuce, endive, radishes, watercress, romaine) for salads.
- Dicing apples, pears, canned fruits.
- Preparing potatoes for French frying, hashed brown, scalloping.
- Dicing celery, carrots, onions, potatoes, all greens, peppers, green beans, turnips, parsnips, beets.
- Cubing bread for stuffing, puddings.
- Chopping nuts, raisins, candied fruits.
- Dicing cooked meats, fowl.

Trimmer

Directions for Use:

1. Grasp handle of the Trimmer between thumb and forefinger of right hand with fingers following curve of handle.

2. The Trimmer is held in the same position regardless of the task: slicing, cutting, trimming, coring, boning, scraping.

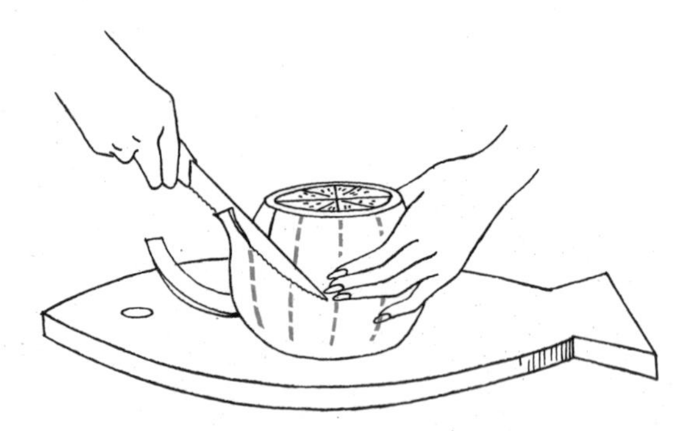

Uses:

- Slicing tomatoes, oranges, cucumbers, hard boiled eggs, green peppers, peaches, pears.
- Cutting and sectioning grapefruit, oranges.
- Making celery curls, carrot sticks; cutting corn from cob.
- Trimming cauliflower, broccoli.
- Peeling pineapple, grapefruit, oranges, melons, eggplant, squash.
- Coring lettuce, green peppers.
- Boning rib roasts, steak, fish, fowl.
- Removing tough outer rind, gristle and excess fat from steaks, chops, roasts; blood vessels from heart; membrane from sweetbreads, kidneys.
- Scraping steaks, roasts, skin of fish before cooking.
- Removing fins from fish; pinfeathers from chickens.
- Gashing edges of steaks, chops, ham slices before broiling.

Butcher Knife

Directions for Use:

1. Place food to be cut on cutting board.

2. Grasp handle of Butcher Knife between thumb and forefinger of right hand with fingers following curve of handle.

3. Place portion of blade nearest to handle of Butcher Knife on food to be cut.

4. Pull back on knife at same time pressing downward, using a long firm stroke. Never cut through bone.

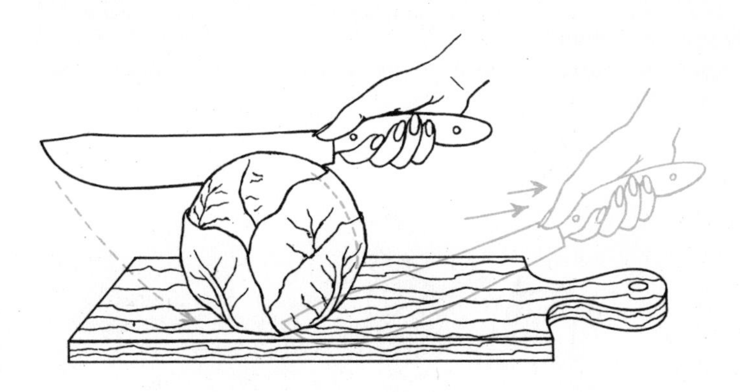

Uses:

- Disjointing chicken, turkey, duck.
- Preparing pork loin; preparing spare ribs.
- Cutting short ribs from rib roast.
- Cutting chuck roast, rump, brisket.
- Cutting squash, pumpkin, rutabaga, cabbage, watermelon, sweet potatoes.
- Cutting lobster, crawfish.
- Removing head of fish, scaling fish.

Carving Knife

Directions for Use:

1. Place meat or fowl to be carved on platter.

2. Grasp handle of Carving Knife between thumb and forefinger of right hand with fingers following curve of handle.

3. Grasp handle of Carving Fork in same manner in left hand; insert tines in meat or fowl.

4. Place portion of blade of Carving Knife nearest to handle on meat or fowl to be carved.

5. Pull back on knife at same time pressing firmly downward to cut through the meat, using a long sweeping stroke rather than a sawing motion.

6. When cutting layer cake, use a long sweeping stroke along with a gentle downward pressure.

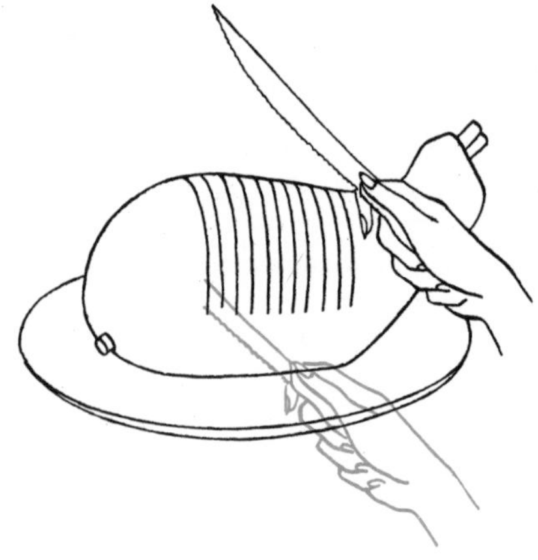

Uses:

- Carving all roasts with bone such as Standing Ribs of Beef, Leg of Lamb, Pork Loin, Baked Ham.
- Carving Turkey, Chicken, Duck, Wild Game.
- Cutting layer cake.

The Slicer

Directions for Use:

1. Place boneless meat or other food to be sliced on cutting board.

2. Grasp handle of The Slicer between thumb and forefinger of right hand with fingers following curve of handle.

3. Place portion of blade of The Slicer nearest to handle on food to be sliced.

4. Pull back on knife with a long sweeping stroke, at the same time exerting a gentle downward pressure. Never use a sawing motion.

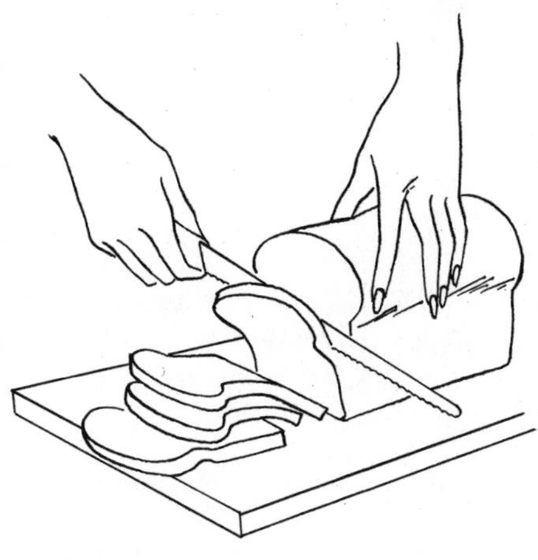

Uses:

- Slicing rolled roasts, white meat of fowl, ham loaf, ham and other boneless meats.
- Slicing all kinds of cheese, eggplant.
- Cutting bread, sandwiches, layer cake.
- Shredding cabbage, lettuce.

• CUTCO •

Paring Knife

Directions for Use:

1. Hold food to be pared firmly in fingers and thumb of left hand.

2. Lay Paring Knife across fingers of right hand with cutting edge of knife pointed to the left. Allow fingers to follow the curve of the handle.

3. Place the thumb of the right hand gently against food to be pared.

4. Make a cut through the skin of the food to be pared; continue cutting a thin layer of the skin using the right thumb to rotate the food and guide the blade of the knife.

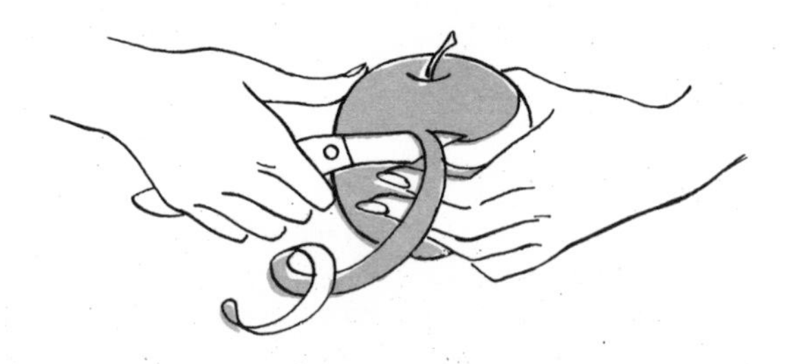

Uses:

- Paring potatoes, apples, cucumbers, peaches, pears, parsnips, turnips, rutabaga.
- Removing roots and stems from carrots, beets, rhubarb, radishes, spinach, cauliflower, celery.
- Scaling asparagus, trimming Brussels sprouts, scraping carrots.
- Cutting eyes from potatoes and blemishes from fruits.
- Pitting plums, peaches, nectarines, pomegranates.
- Seeding and skinning grapes.
- Making radish roses, celery curls, pickle fans.
- Removing black line from shrimp.
- Removing stomach sac from lobster.

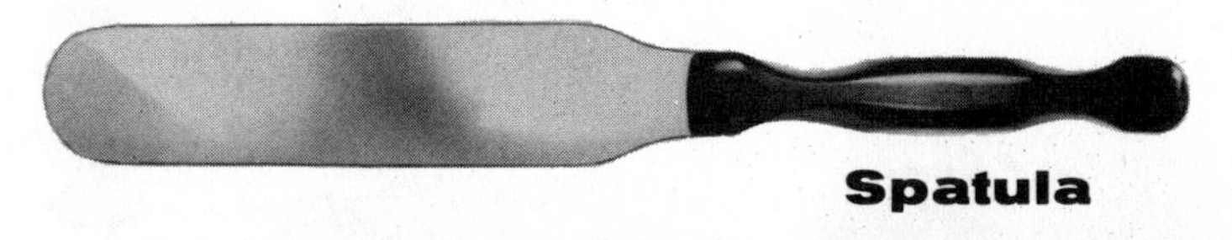

Spatula

Carving Fork

Turning Fork

Directions for Use:

Grasp handle of the Spatula, Carving Fork or Turning Fork between thumb and forefinger of right hand with fingers following curve of handle.

Uses:

Spatula:

- Turning meat patties, fish, breaded meats.
- Turning potato cakes, stirring hashed brown potatoes.
- Serving meat patties, fried eggs, potato cakes, pancakes, omelets.
- Icing cakes, cookies.
- Removing cookies from baking sheet or corn bread from pan.
- Removing food from mixing bowl.
- Leveling cups of flour, sugar; mixing dry ingredients for baking.
- Removing ice cream from paper carton.
- Loosening ice cube trays from freezer compartment.
- Turning fruits (peaches, apricots, pineapple) and vegetables (tomatoes, eggplant) as they are broiled or sauteed.
- Perfect for lifting that first piece of pie from the plate.

Carving Fork:

- Turning large roasts or turkeys.
- Holding large roasts or turkeys in place during carving.

Turning Fork:

- Turning bacon, liver, steaks, chops, fried chicken, ham, fish.
- Serving meats, fish or fowl.
- Removing beets, turnips, rutabaga, sauerkraut, corn on the cob, spinach from cooking utensil.

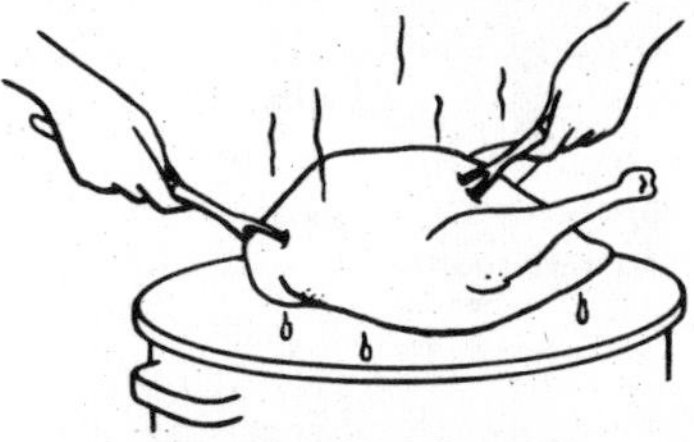

Turning Fork and Carving Fork together:

- Lifting large roasts or turkey from the roasting pan to the serving platter.

7 Methods of Cooking Meat

There are seven specific methods of cooking meat. It may be cooked by roasting, broiling, panbroiling or griddle broiling, panfrying, deep fat frying, braising and cooking in water. The cut of the meat usually determines the cooking method.

HOW TO ROAST

Any tender cut of beef, veal, pork or lamb may be roasted as follows:

1. Season as desired. It makes little difference whether a roast is salted before or after cooking because when done, the salt has penetrated only to a depth of about one half inch.

2. Place meat fat side up on rack in an open roasting pan. The rack holds the roast out of the drippings and with fat on top, roast will do its own basting.

3. Insert a meat thermometer so that its bulb is in the center of the thickest part. The bulb should not rest on the fat or touch the bone. If no meat thermometer is available, the oven temperature should be 325° F.

4. Add no water; do not cover. Roasting is a dry heat method of cooking. If the pan is covered or water added, the meat will be a pot roast.

5. Roast in slow oven, 325° F. The oven may be started just as the roast is put in.

6. Roast to the desired degree of doneness.

HOW TO BROIL

Tender beef steaks, lamb or mutton chops, sliced ham or bacon and ground beef or lamb are suitable for broiling. Fresh pork and veal are seldom broiled. Steaks and chops should be cut at least one inch thick for best broiling and a slice of ham at least one half inch thick. To broil:

1. Turn oven regulator to "broil." Preheat or not as desired.

2. Line broiler pan with Alcoa Wrap.

3. Place meat on rack of broiler pan, 2-3 inches from the heat; the thicker the meat the greater the distance from the heat.

4. Broil until top side is thoroughly browned; season with salt, pepper (except ham, bacon).

5. Turn; brown second side; season; serve at once.

HOW TO PANBROIL

The same tender cuts of meat suitable for broiling may also be panbroiled. An aluminum fry pan or griddle is particularly good for this type of broiling.

1. Place pan over medium high heat.

2. Place small piece of white paper in bottom of pan. When paper turns a golden brown, add meat; reduce heat to medium. When the cold meat hits the hot pan it will stick but as it cooks and browns it will loosen itself. If juices start to cook out of the meat, increase heat slightly.

3. When meat is brown on one side, turn; brown second side. Do not cover and do not add water.

4. When meat is cooked to desired degree of doneness, season and serve at once.

HOW TO PAN FRY

Comparatively thin pieces of tender meat, meat that has been made tender by pounding, cubing, scoring or grinding, or meat that is breaded is best suited to panfrying which is the cooking of meat in a small amount of fat. To panfry:

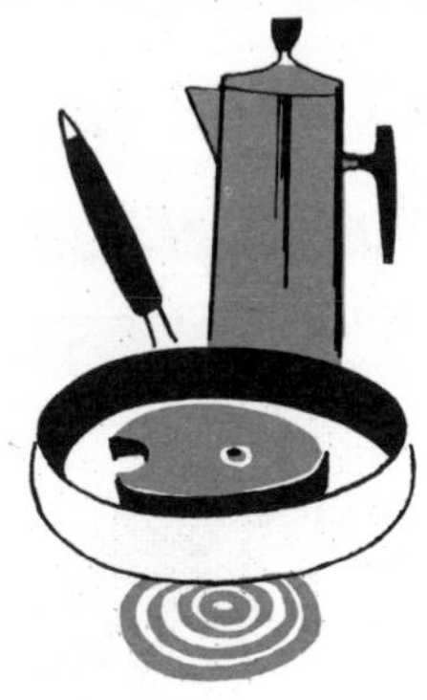

1. Place fry pan over medium high heat; add small amount of fat—usually two tablespoons will be sufficient.

2. When fat starts to bubble or sputter, add meat; cook as in pan-broiling.

HOW TO DEEP FAT FRY

This method of cooking is almost always used for breaded meats or croquettes made from leftovers. To deep fat fry:

1. Place about one pound fat in French fryer or a deep kettle. Heat fat to correct temperature. Most accurate temperature control is obtained by using a thermometer. Temperatures for deep fat frying of meat range from 300° to 350° F., dependent upon size of pieces and whether it is uncooked or left over meat.

2. Place a few pieces of meat in fry basket; lower slowly into hot fat.

3. If fat covers meat, no turning is necessary; allow meat to brown thoroughly and cook through.

4. When done, raise basket; let meat drain; remove from basket.

5. In this type of frying, best results are obtained when only a few pieces are fried at one time.

6. Fat may be used again if it is strained and stored in refrigerator.

HOW TO BRAISE

Braising, also known as pot roasting, is the method most frequently used for cooking the less tender cuts of meat. Some tender cuts are also better if braised. These include pork chops, pork steaks, pork cutlets, veal chops, veal steaks, veal cutlets and pork liver. To braise:

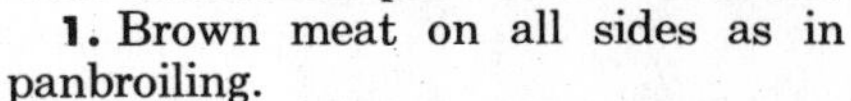

1. Brown meat on all sides as in panbroiling.

2. When brown, season; cover; reduce heat to low; cook until tender, turning frequently.

3. Use covered roaster for larger pieces of meat such as chuck, shoulder, rump or brisket; a fry pan or Dutch Oven for smaller cuts. Aluminum utensils require no added water; meats will cook in their own juices.

HOW TO COOK IN WATER

Large cuts of meat may be browned or not as desired. However, browning helps to develop flavor and improves the color. Corned beef and cured pork need not be browned.

1. Brown meat on all sides.

2. Cover with water or stock; liquid may be hot or cold—it makes no difference.

3. Season with salt, pepper, spices and vegetables.

4. Cover; simmer until tender.

Small pieces of meat such as are used in stews are prepared as follows:

1. Cut meat into 1 inch cubes; roll in seasoned flour; brown on all sides in hot fat.

2. Add just enough water, stock or vegetable juice to cover meat.

3. Season as desired; cover; simmer until meat is tender.

4. Vegetables are added about one hour before cooking time is completed. Liquid is thickened just before serving.

Beef Cuts THEIR APPEARAN

BLADE POT ROAST CHUCK

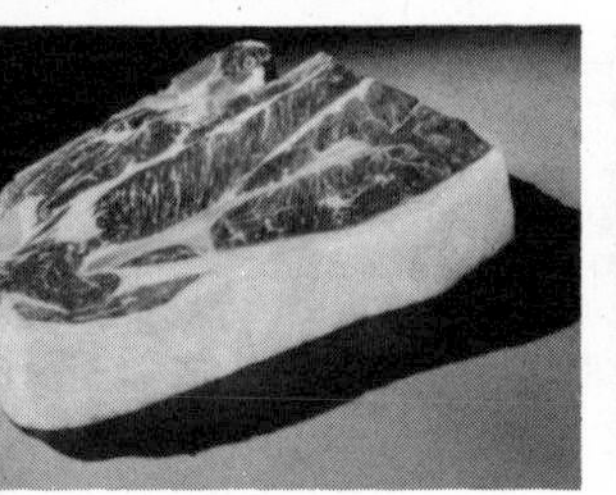

Braise

STANDING RIB

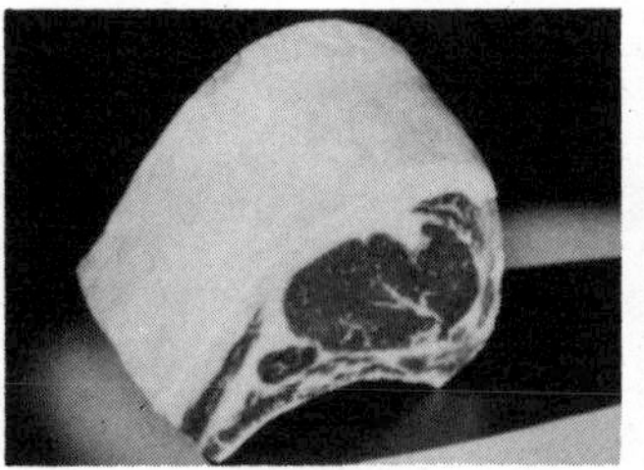

Roast

PORTERHOUSE STEA

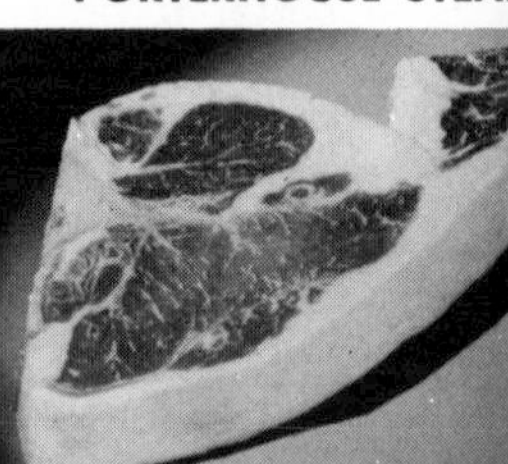

Broil, Panbroil, Panf

ARM POT ROAST CHUCK

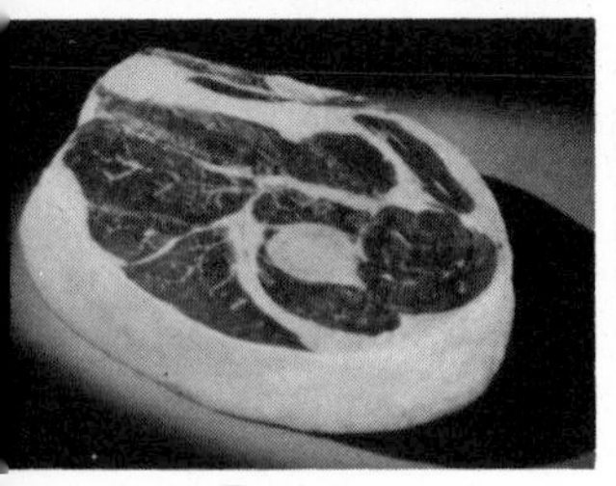

Braise

RIB STEAK

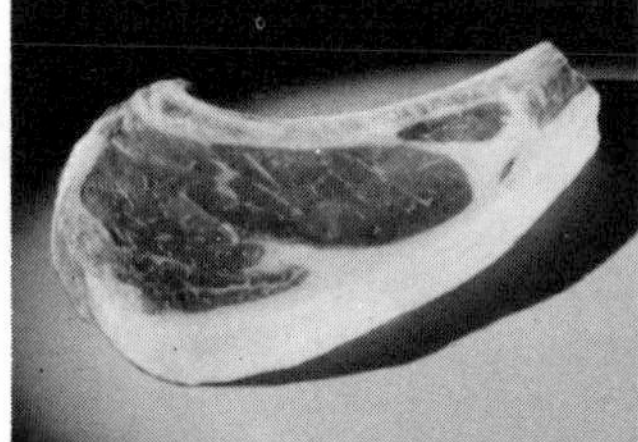

Broil, Panbroil, Panfry

T-BONE STEAK

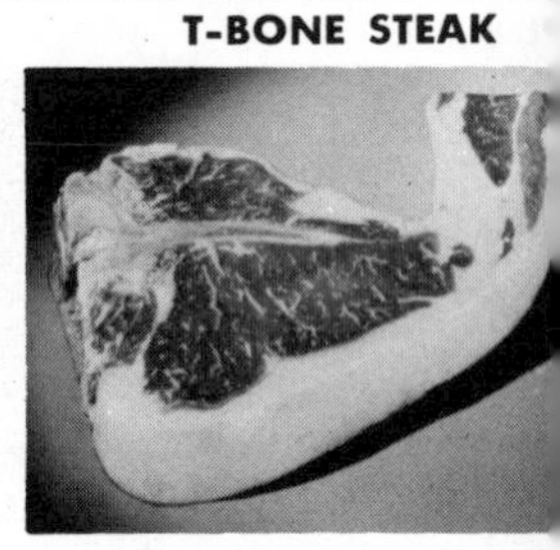

Broil, Panbroil, Panf

BONELESS CHUCK

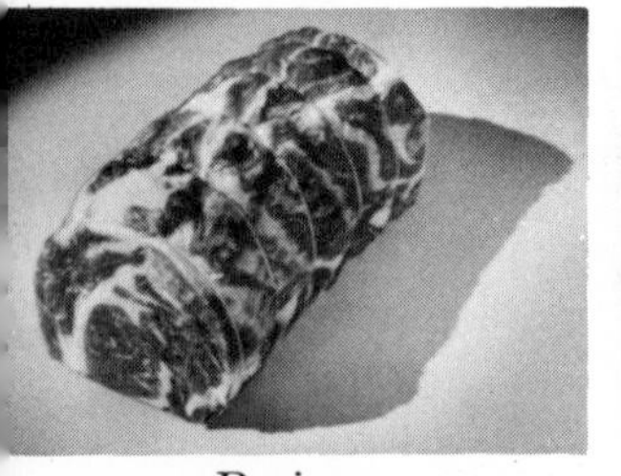

Braise

ROLLED RIB

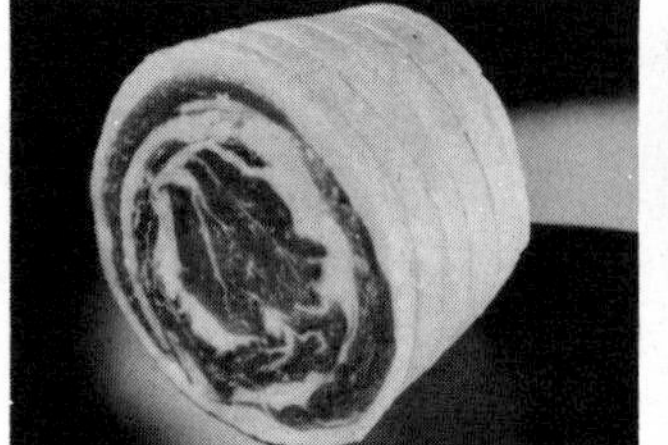

Roast

CLUB STEAK

Broil, Panbroil, Panf

SHANK CROSS CUTS

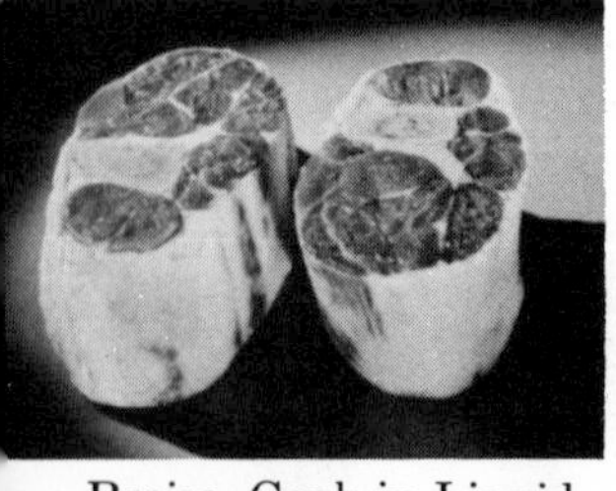

Braise, Cook in Liquid

BRISKET—BONE IN

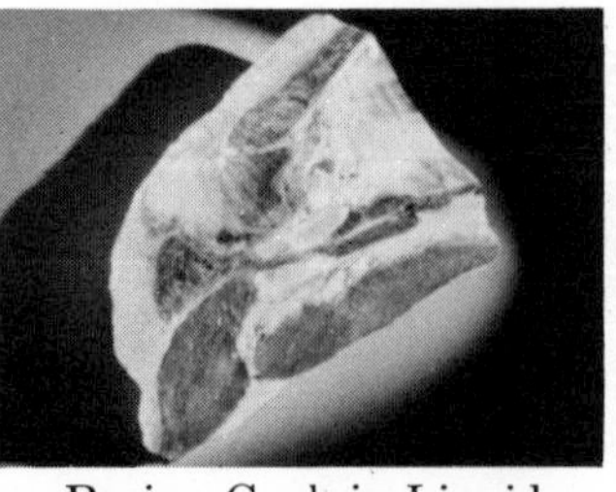
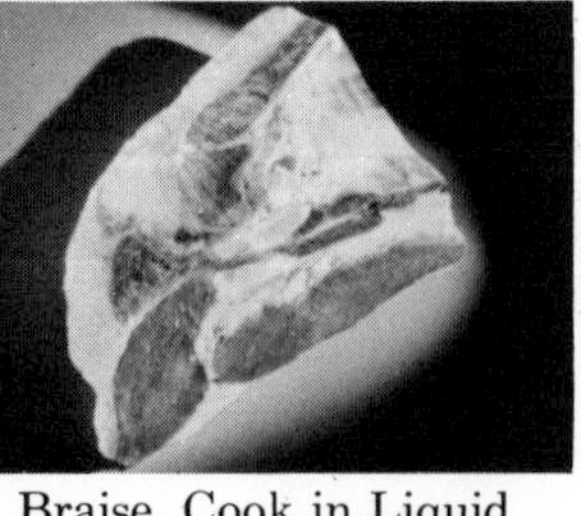

Braise, Cook in Liquid

CORNED BEEF—BRISK

Cook in Liquid

Courtesy of the National Live Stock and Meat Boar

ND HOW TO COOK THEM

Courtesy of the National Live Stock and Meat Board

Veal Cuts THEIR APPEARANC

ARM ROAST—SHOULDER

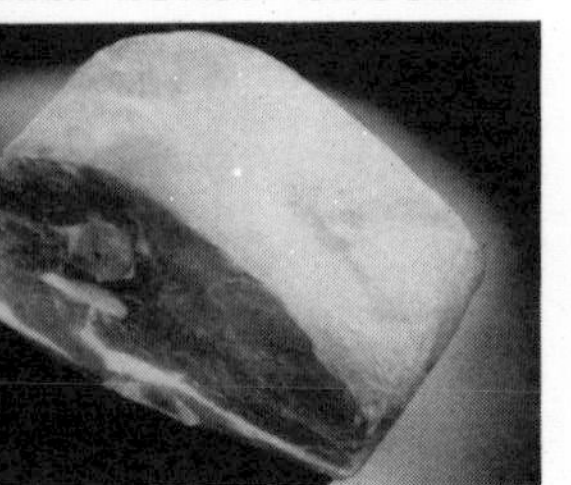

Roast, Braise

BLADE ROAST—SHOULDER

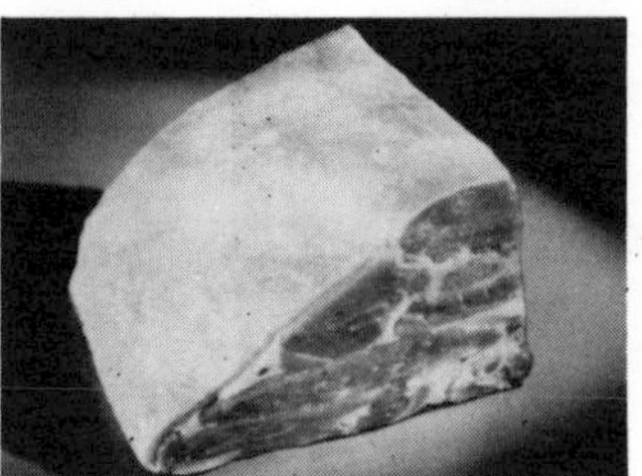

Roast, Braise

RIB ROAST

Roast, Braise

ARM STEAK—SHOULDER

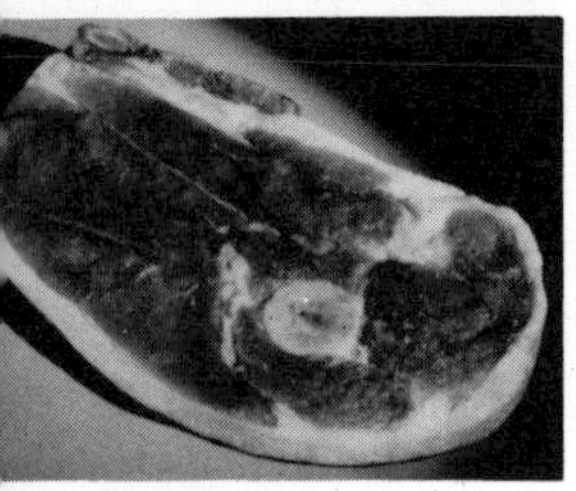

Braise, Panfry

BLADE STEAK—SHOULDER

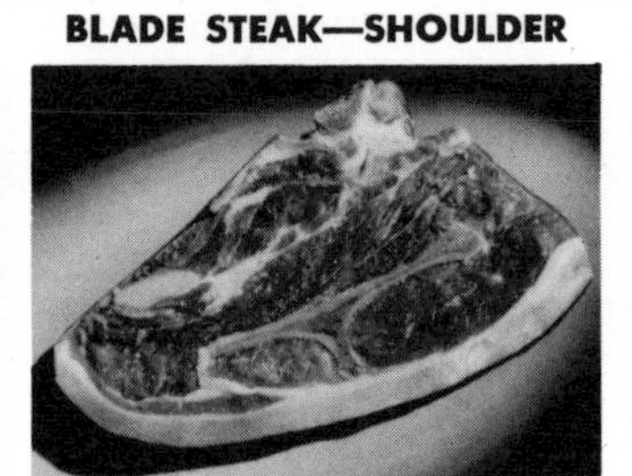

Braise, Panfry

RIB CHOP

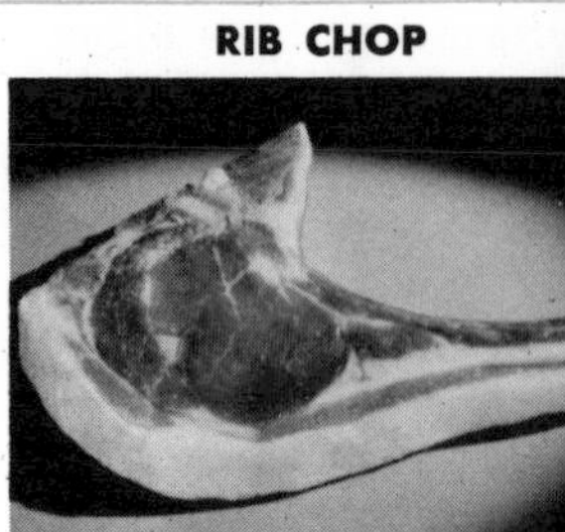

Braise, Panfry

ROLLED SHOULDER

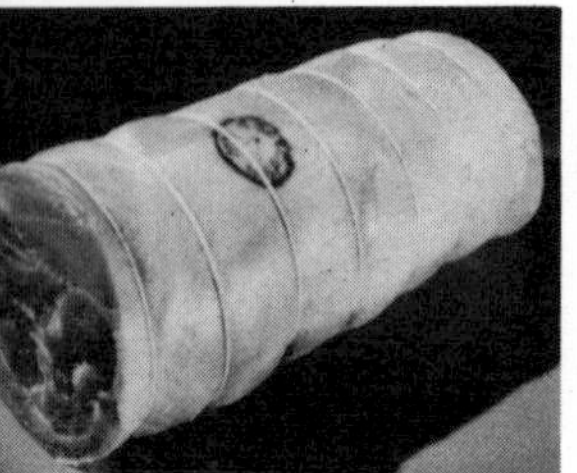

Roast, Braise

BREAST

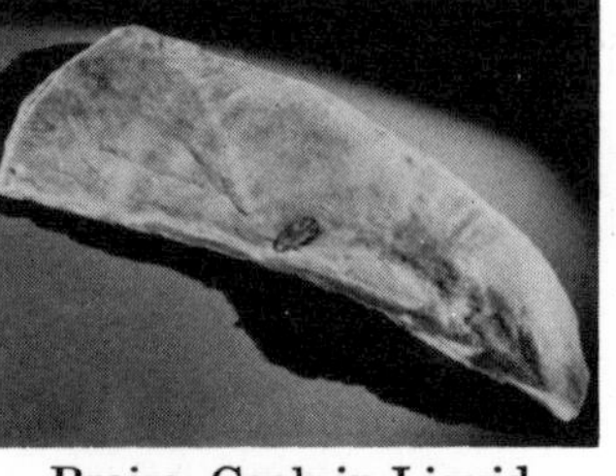

Braise, Cook in Liquid

RIBLETS, BREAST

Braise, Cook in Liquid

FORESHANK

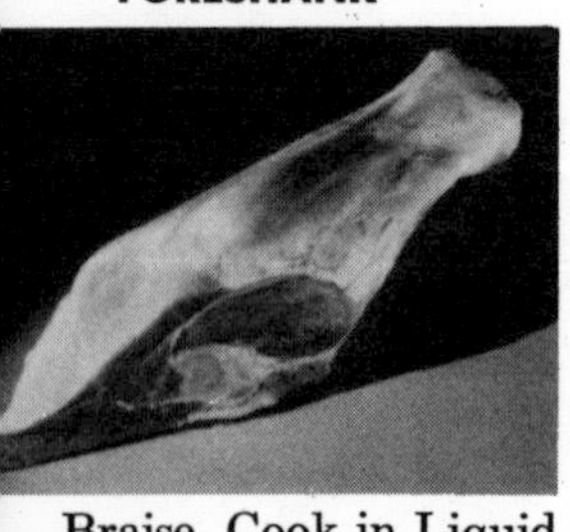

Braise, Cook in Liquid

CITY CHICKEN

Braise

MOCK CHICKEN LEGS

Braise

Courtesy of the National Live Stock and Meat Board

ND HOW TO COOK THEM

STANDING RUMP	CENTER CUT OF LEG	SHANK HALF OF LEG
Roast, Braise	Roast, Braise	Roast, Braise
BONELESS RUMP	**HEEL OF ROUND**	**ROUNDSTEAK—CUTLET**
Roast, Braise	Roast, Braise, Cook in Liquid	Braise, Panfry
SIRLOIN ROAST	**SIRLOIN STEAK**	**BONELESS STEW**
Roast, Braise	Braise, Panfry	Cook in Liquid
LOIN ROAST	**LOIN CHOP**	**KIDNEY CHOP**
Roast, Braise	Braise, Panfry	Braise, Panfry

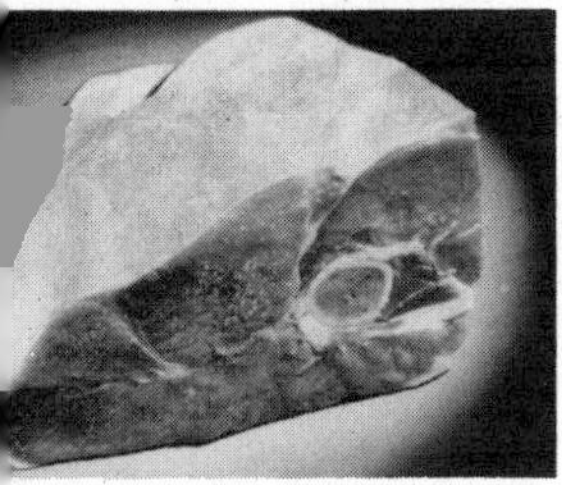

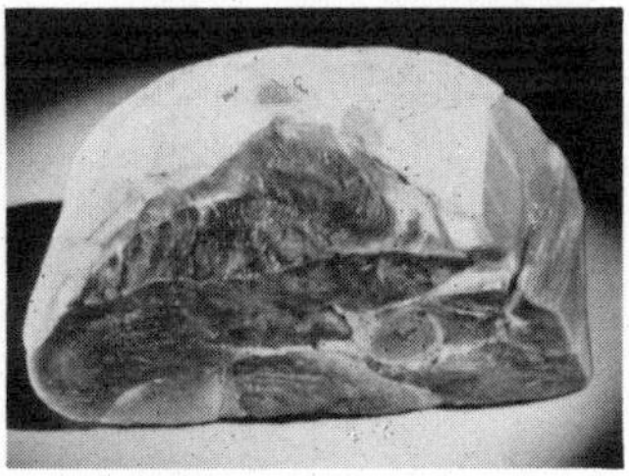

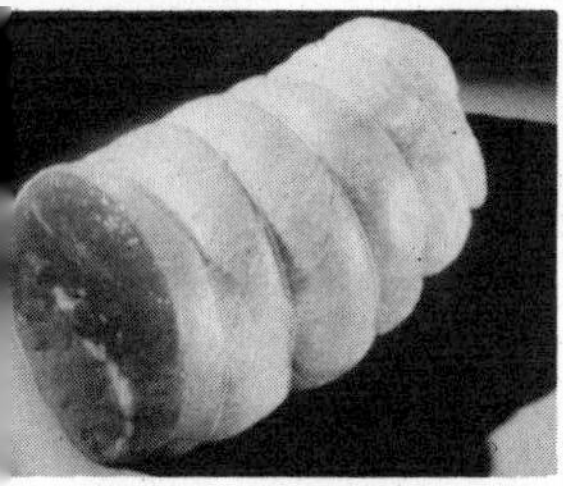

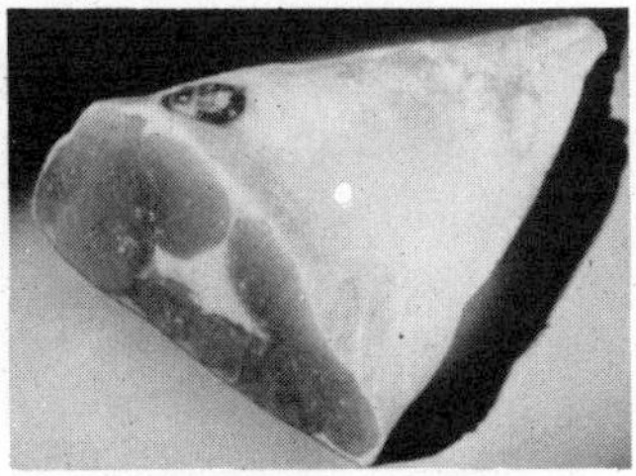

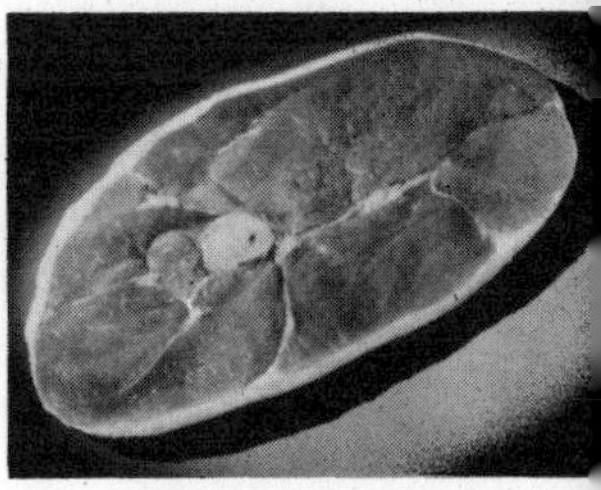

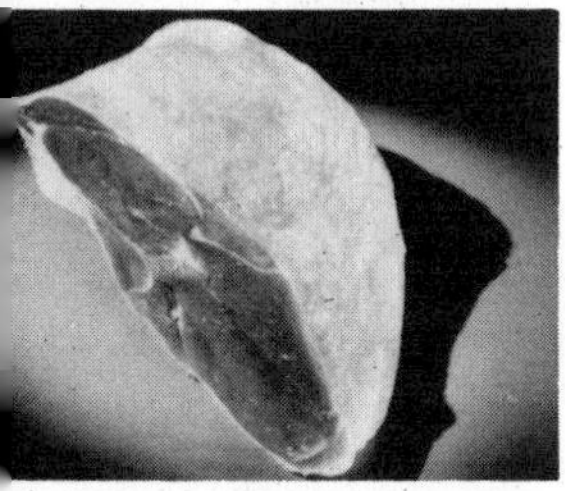

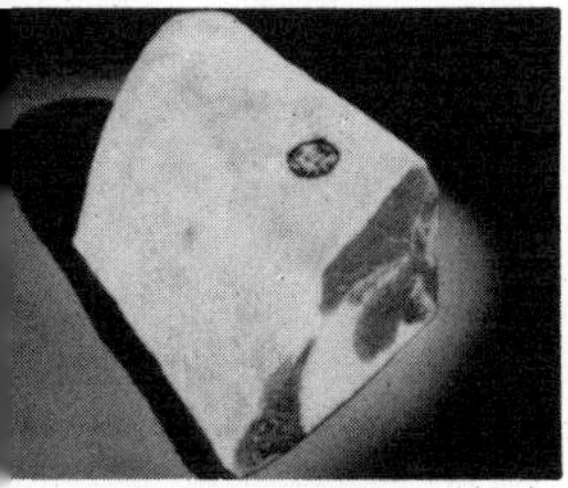

Courtesy of the National Live Stock and Meat Board

Pork Cuts THEIR APPEARANC

BOSTON BUTT—SHOULDER

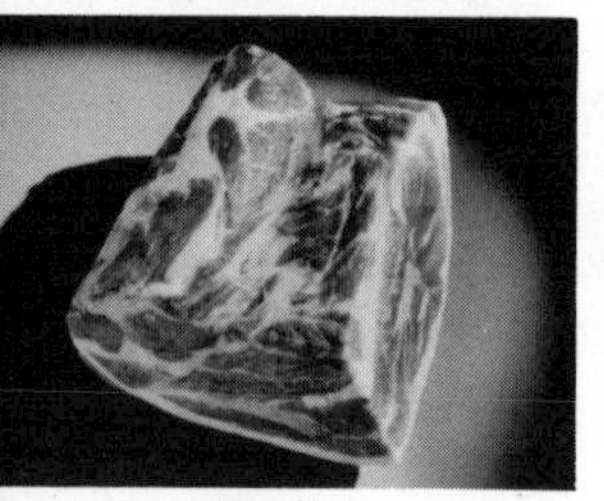

Roast

BLADE LOIN ROAST

Roast

LOIN ROAST—CENTER C

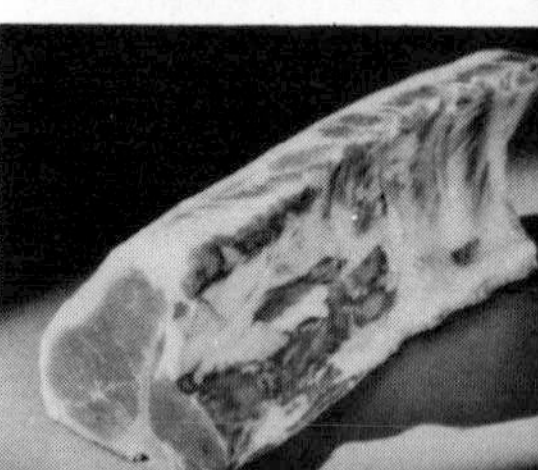

Roast

BLADE STEAK—SHOULDER

Braise, Panfry

FRESH PICNIC SHOULDER

Roast

LOIN CHOPS

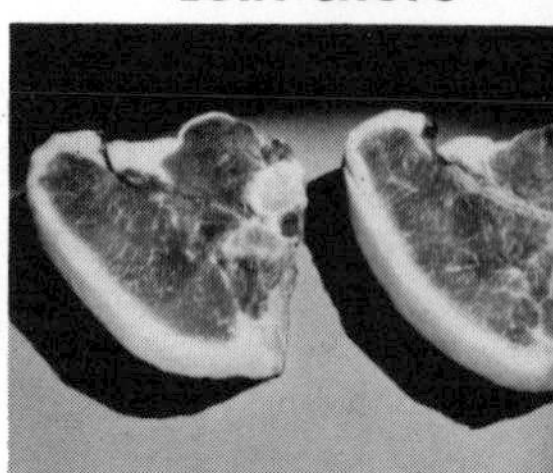

Braise, Panfry

ARM ROAST—SHOULDER

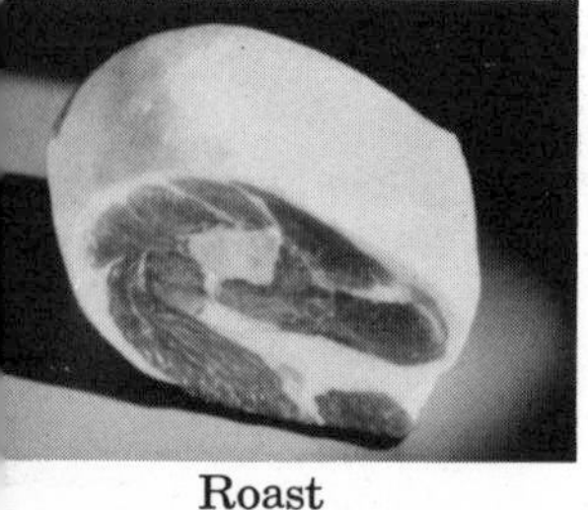

Roast

SMOKED PICNIC SHOULDER

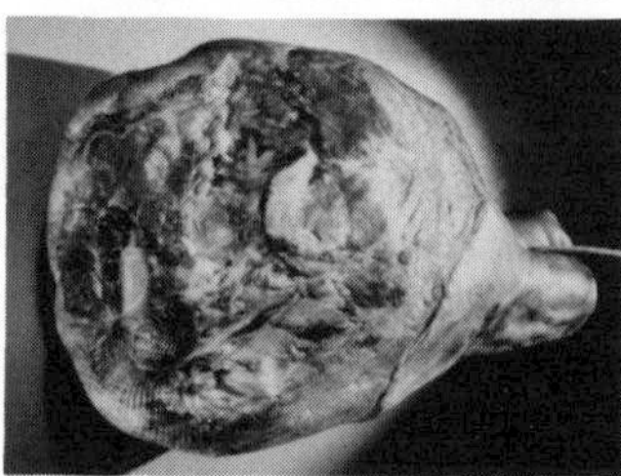

Roast, Cook in Liquid

RIB CHOPS

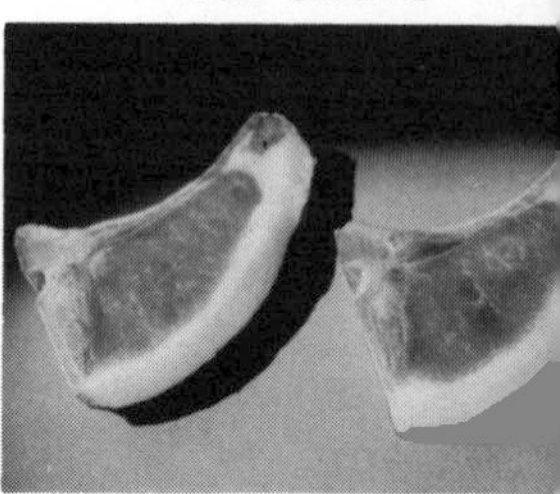

Braise, Panfry

ARM STEAK—SHOULDER

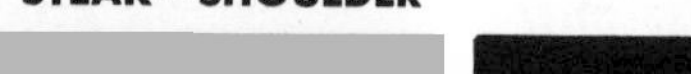

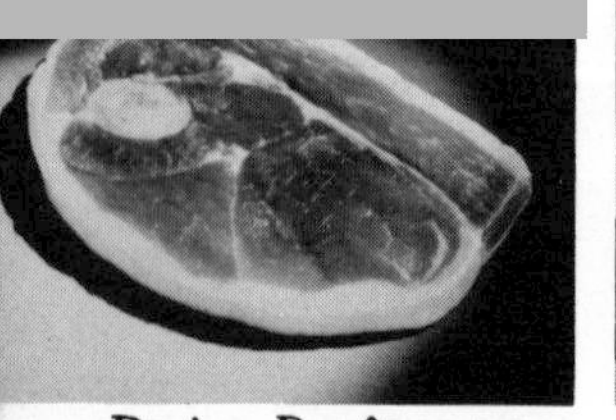

Braise, Panfry

HOCKS

Braise, Cook in Liquid

CROWN ROAST

Roast

D HOW TO COOK THEM

SPARERIBS

st, Braise, Cook in Liquid

HALF HAM—SHANK END

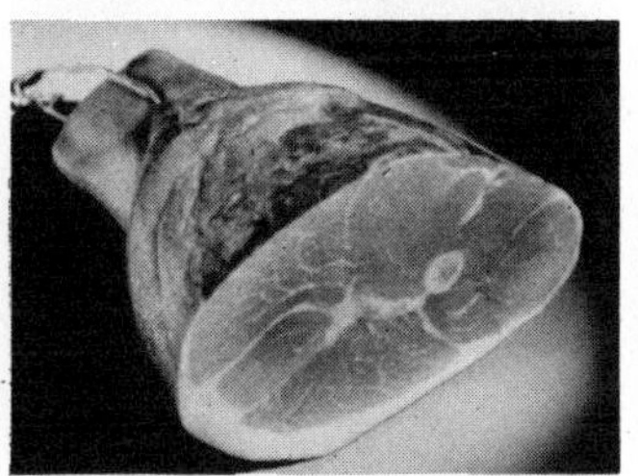

Roast, Cook in Liquid

HALF HAM—BUTT END

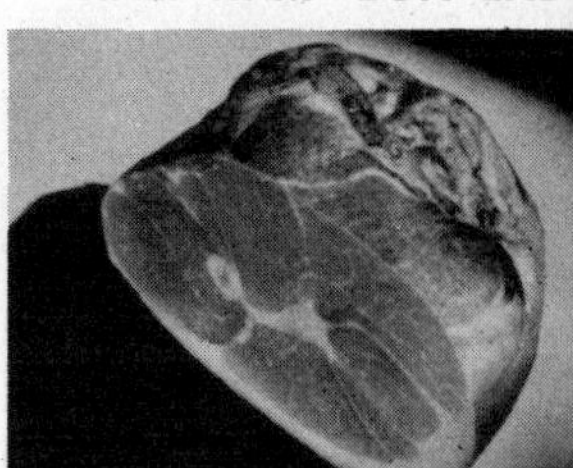

Roast, Cook in Liquid

TENDERLOIN

Roast, Braise, Panfry

HAM CENTER SLICE

Broil, Panbroil, Panfry

SLICED BACON

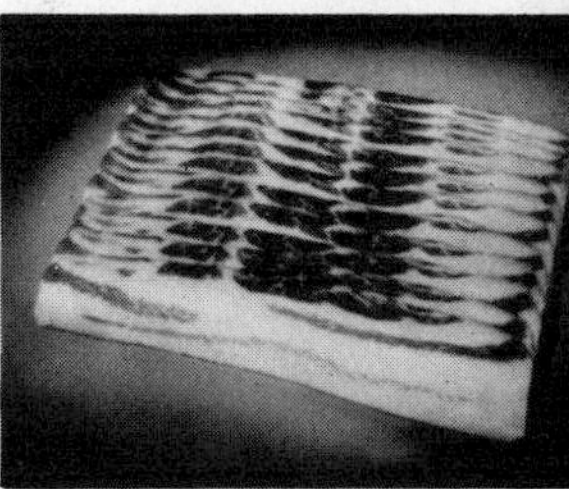

Broil, Panbroil

NELESS SIRLOIN ROAST

Roast

JOWL BACON SQUARE

Panbroil, Panfry Cook in Liquid, Broil

SALT PORK—SIDE

Cook in Liquid, Panbroil

ANADIAN STYLE BACON

ast, Broil, Panfry, Panbroil

SMOKED SHOULDER BUTT

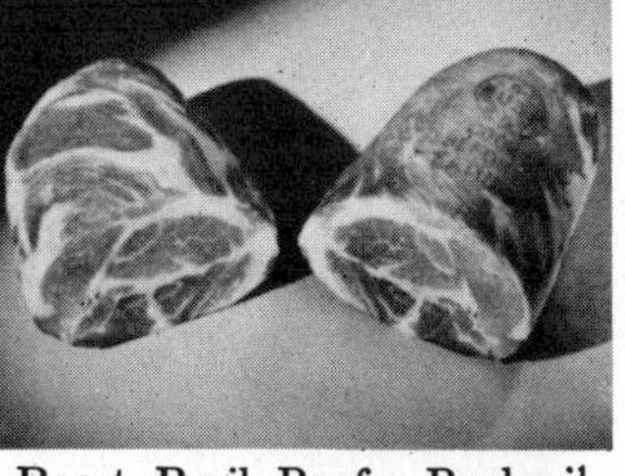

Roast, Broil, Panfry, Panbroil

SIRLOIN ROAST

Roast

Courtesy of the National Live Stock and Meat Board

Lamb Cuts THEIR APPEARANC

SHOULDER SQUARE CUT

Roast

SHOULDER CUSHION

Roast

BREAST

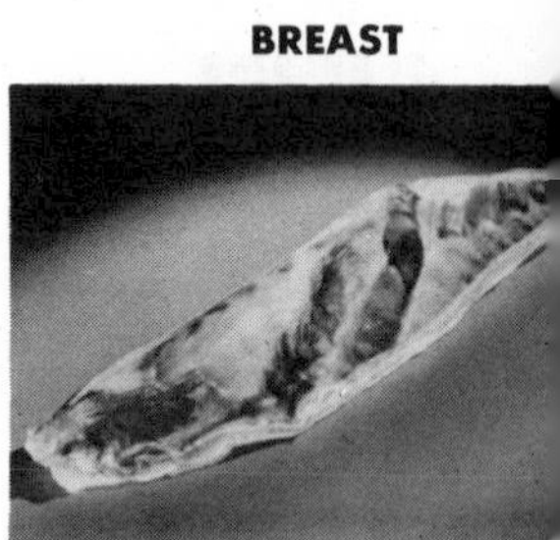

Braise, Roast

SHOULDER CHOPS

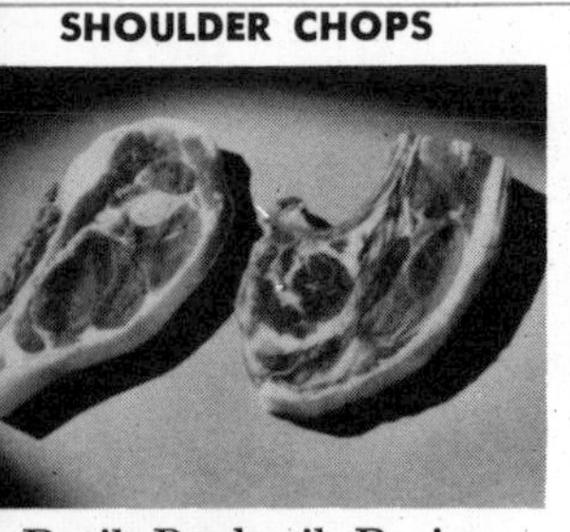

Broil, Panbroil, Braise

ROLLED SHOULDER

Roast, Braise

RIBLETS—BREAST

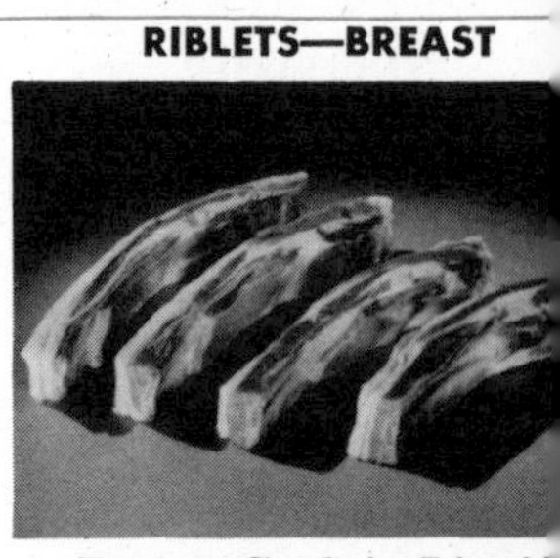

Braise, Cook in Liquic

SARATOGA CHOPS

Broil, Panbroil, Braise

GROUND LAMB

Roast

ROLLED BREAST

Braise, Roast

NECK SLICES

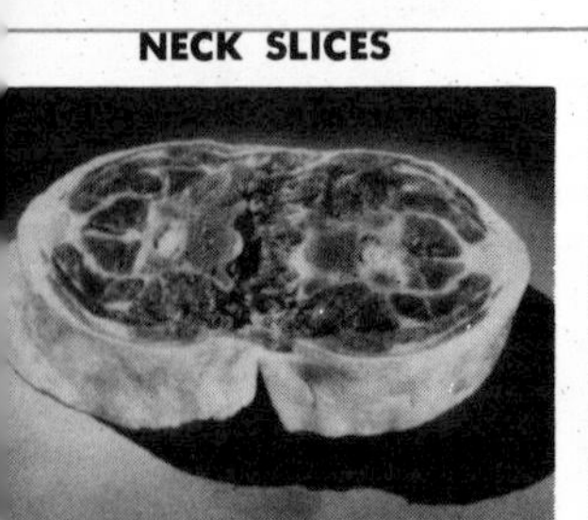

Braise, Cook in Liquid

PATTIES

Broil, Panbroil

SHANKS

Braise, Cook in Liquic

ND HOW TO COOK THEM

RIB ROAST—RACK

Roast

LOIN ROAST

Roast

FRENCHED LEG

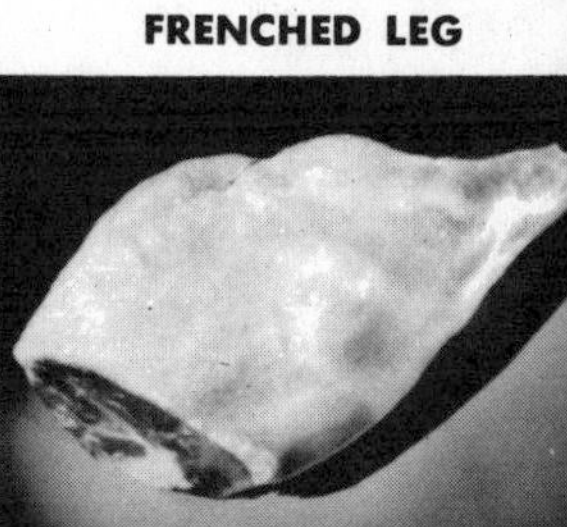

Roast

RIB CHOPS

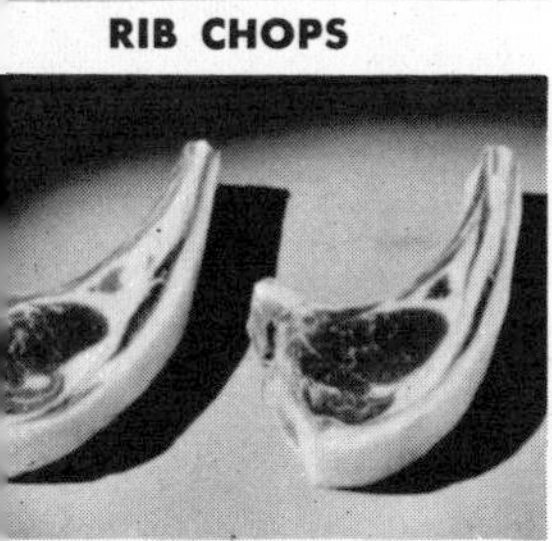

Broil, Panbroil

LOIN CHOPS

Broil, Panbroil

AMERICAN LEG

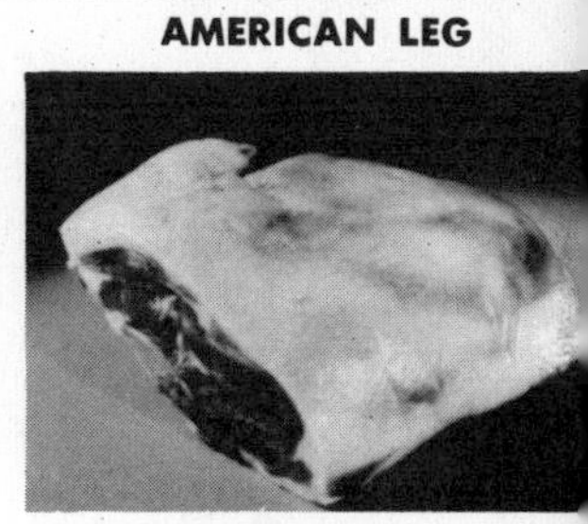

Roast

ELESS SIRLOIN ROAST

Roast

ROLLED LOIN

Roast

CROWN ROAST

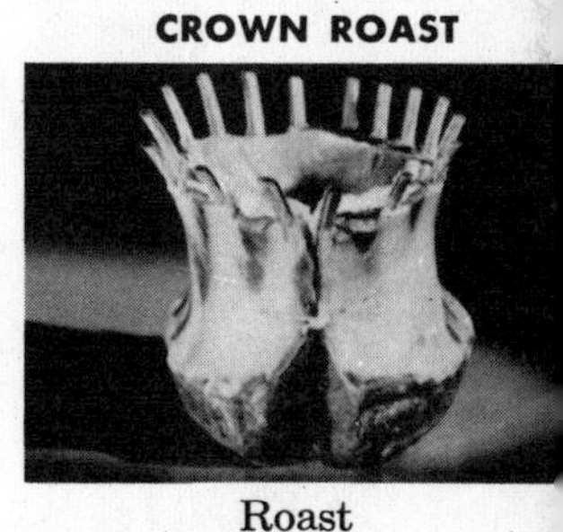

Roast

FRENCHED CHOPS

Broil, Panbroil

ENGLISH CHOPS

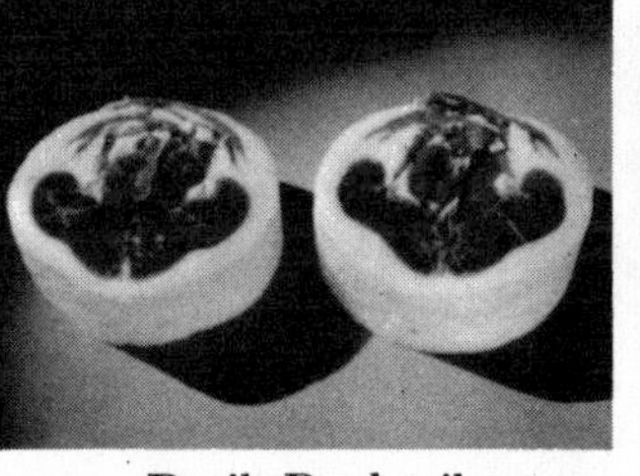

Broil, Panbroil

SIRLOIN CHOPS

Broil, Panbroil

Courtesy of the National Live Stock and Meat Board

Variety Meats THEIR APPEARANC AND HOW TO COOK THEM

SWEETBREADS

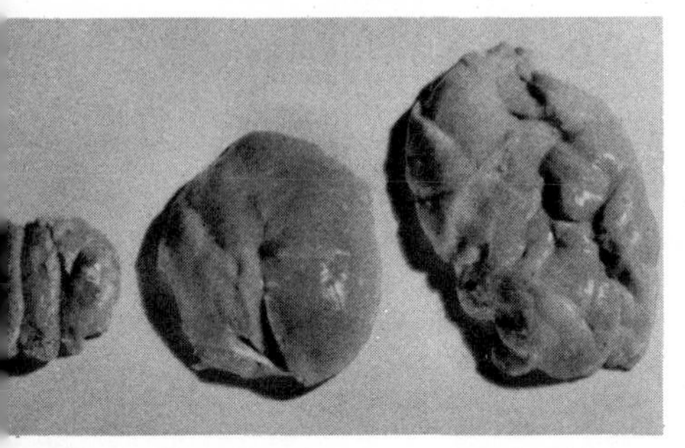

Broil, Fry, Braise, Cook in Liquid

TONGUES

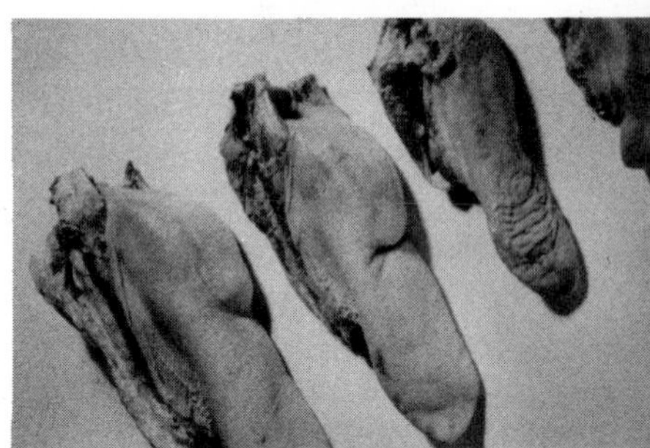

Cook in Liquid

BRAINS

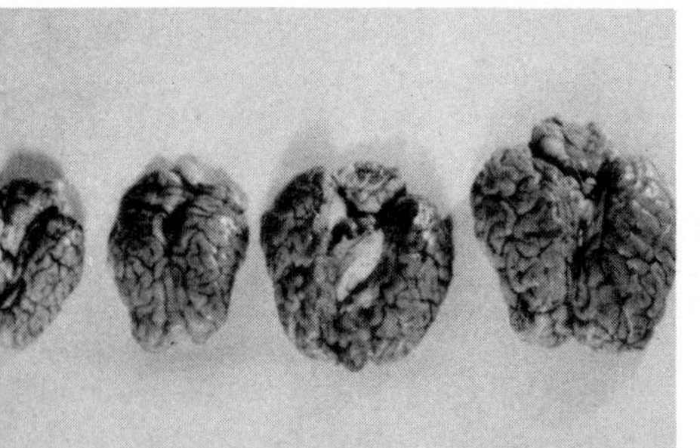

Broil, Fry, Braise, Cook in Liquid

HEARTS

Braise, Cook in Liquid

LIVERS

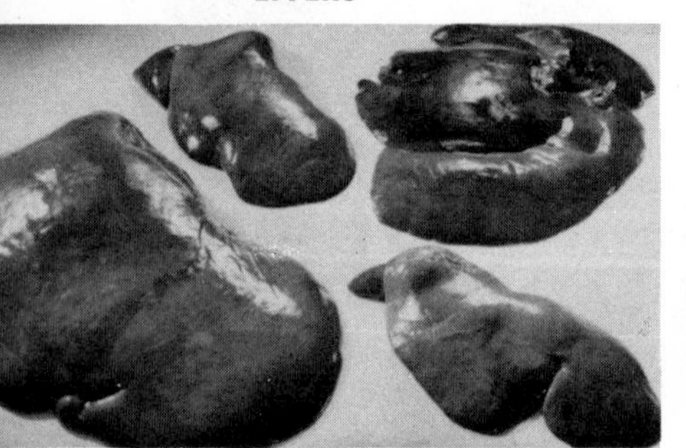

Beef, Pork: Roast, Braise, Fry
Veal, Lamb: Broil, Panbroil, Fry

KIDNEYS

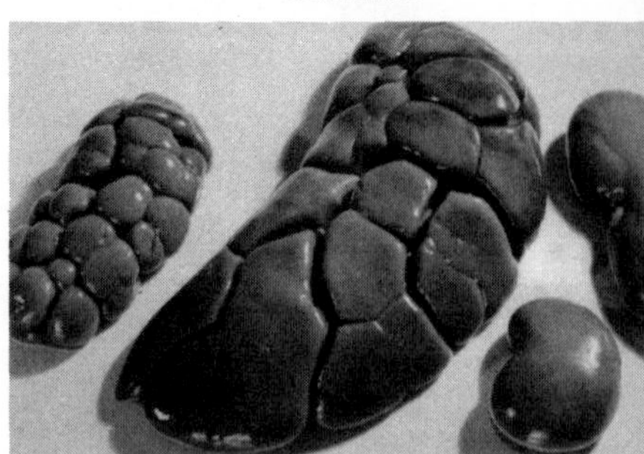

Beef, Pork: Braise, Cook in Liquid
Veal, Lamb: Broil, Panbroil, Braise, Cook in Liquid

Courtesy of the National Live Stock and Meat Boar

Buying Guide FOR MEAT, POULTRY

	CHARACTERISTICS	CUT	WEIGHT	NUMBER OF SERVINGS
Beef	Color, purplish brown when first cut, changing rapidly to bright cherry red when exposed to air; lean, firm, fine grained, well marbled with fat; bones red, porous; fat white, brittle, flaky.	Short Ribs	1 lb.	1–2
		Sirloin Steak	1 lb.	1–3
		Round Steak	1 lb.	2–3
		Standing Rib	5 lbs.	8–10
		Boneless, Stewing	1 lb.	3–4
		Hamburger	1 lb.	3–4
		Brisket	1 lb.	2–3
		Flank Steak	1 lb.	2–3
Pork, fresh	Color, light greyish pink; lean, firm, fine grained; well marbled with fat; fat white, firm, free from fibers; bones slightly pink.	Spareribs	1½ lbs.	2
		Loin Roast	4 lbs.	7–8
		Fresh Ham	12 lbs.	20–24
		Chops, thick	1 lb.	2
		Sausages	1 lb.	8–16 sausages
Pork, smoked	Color, rich pink; lean, fine grained, well marbled with fat; a good layer of fat on outside; bone small.	Shoulder Picnic Ham	6 lbs.	9–10
		Whole Ham	12 lbs.	20–24
		Ham Slice	1 lb.	2–3
		Bacon	1 lb.	20–24 slices
Lamb	Color, dull pink; lean, firm, fine grained, tender, well marbled with fat; fat firm, white, thin, weblike; bones soft, red.	Chops, thick	1 lb.	2
		Leg-Roast	6 lbs.	10–12
		Shoulder-Roast	4 lbs.	7–8
		Breast	1 lb.	2
		Shanks	1 lb.	1–2
Veal	Color, light greyish pink; lean, firm, fine grained, well marked with fat; fat white, firm, free from fiber; bones slightly pink.	Chops, thick	1 lb.	2
		Steaks	1 lb.	2–3
		Leg-Roast	4 lbs.	6–8
		Shoulder-Roast	2 lbs.	3–4
Chicken Capon Turkey	Skin smooth, unbroken, moist; legs smooth, soft; fat distributed evenly; breast bone pliable.	Broilers	¼–½ bird	1
		Fryers	¾ lb.	1
		Pieces	¾ lb.	1
		Roasting Chicken	⅔–¾ lb.	1
		Stewing Chicken	⅓–⅔ lb.	6
		Whole Turkey	½–¾ lb.	1
Duck	Breast firm, thick, tender; breastbone and bill pliable.	Whole Duck	¾–1 lb.	1

SUGGESTIONS FOR BEEF

MEAT	SOUP-APPETIZER	STARCHY FOOD	OTHER VEGETABLE
Roast Rib of Beef	Consommé	Baked Potato	Buttered Green Beans
	Frozen Tomato Juice	Browned Potatoes	Broccoli with Hollandaise Sauce
	Grapefruit Half	Mashed Potatoes	Buttered Beets
Rolled Beef Roast	Fruit Cup	Creamed Potatoes	Buttered Carrots
	Beef Bouillon	Corn on Cob	Buttered Cabbage
	Grapefruit Juice	Parsley Potatoes	Green Beans with Pimento
Broiled Steak	Seafood	French Fried Potatoes	Stewed Tomatoes
	Vegetable Juice	Lima Beans with Pimento	Buttered Asparagus
	Onion Soup	Baked Stuffed Potato	Green Beans with Mushrooms
Beef Pot Roast	Melon Ball Cocktail	Mashed Potatoes	Buttered Broccoli
	Cream of Celery Soup	Potato Pancakes	Harvard Beets
	Pineapple Shrub	Buttered Noodles	Browned Carrots
Swiss Steak	Grapefruit Half	Au Gratin Potatoes	Buttered Asparagus
	Mushroom Soup	Mashed Potatoes	Browned Carrots
	Tomato Juice	Boiled Potatoes	Brussels Sprouts
Beef Stew	Fruit Cup	Dumplings	Spinach
	Onion Soup	Rice	Swiss Chard
	Jellied Bouillon	Boiled Potatoes	Peas and Carrots
Corned Beef	Clear Soup	Boiled Potatoes	Cabbage Wedges
	Spinach Soup	Home Fries	Onions and Carrots
	Sauerkraut Juice	Parsley Potatoes	Turnips
Corned Beef Hash	Prune Juice	Potatoes are in the hash	Green Beans
	Mock Turtle Soup		Spinach with Hard Cooked Egg
	Tomato Bisque		Asparagus
Braised Short Ribs	Mixed Fruit Juice	Browned Potatoes	Browned Carrots
	Navy Bean Soup	Riced Potatoes	Braised Celery
	Beef Broth	Hominy Au Gratin	Steamed Cabbage

Menu SUGGESTIONS FOR BEEF

BREAD	ACCOMPANIMENT	SALAD	DESSERT
Soft Rolls	Celery-Olives	Tossed Green	Fresh Fruit
Hard Rolls	Brown Gravy	Jellied Vegetable	Cherry Pie
Gingerbread Muffins	Yorkshire Pudding	Pineapple	Chocolate Cake
Sliced Bread	Horseradish Sauce	Head Lettuce	Chocolate Sundae
Hard Rolls	Pepper Relish	Lettuce-Tomato	Apple Pie
Sally Lunn Squares	Pan Gravy	Mixed Green	Red Raspberry Sherbet
Soft Rolls	Mushroom Gravy	Lettuce with Roquefort Dressing	Lemon Meringue Pie
Sliced Bread	Pickled Onions	Perfection	Chocolate Ice Cream
French Bread	Chili Sauce	Combination	Coconut Cake
Rye Bread	Brown Gravy	Cole Slaw	Rice Pudding
Hard Rolls	Spiced Crabapple	Head Lettuce	Apple Brown Betty
Corn Muffins	Chili Sauce	Fresh Vegetable	Gingerbread
Hard Rolls	Pickled Onions	Mixed Green	Pumpkin Pie
Sliced Bread	Applesauce	Tomato-Cucumber	Pineapple Sherbet
Salted Rye Rolls	Spiced Peach	Waldorf	Baked Lemon Custard
Toasted Rolls	Celery Hearts	Cole Slaw	Ice Cream
Sliced Bread	Pickled Pears	Head Lettuce	Spice Cake
Melba Toast	Horseradish	Mixed Green	Chocolate Cake
Poppyseed Rolls	Mustard Sauce	Head Lettuce	Fruit
White Bread	Horseradish Sauce	Celery-Radish	Blueberry Pie
Corn Bread	Dill Pickles	Stuffed Prunes	Peach Tapioca
Hard Rolls	Chili Sauce	Fresh Vegetable	Sliced Bananas
Graham Bread	Piccalilli	Lettuce-Tomato	Butterscotch Pudding
French Bread	Cranberry Jelly	Mixed Green	Washington Pie
Crusty Rolls	Pickle Relish	Jellied Vegetable	Cottage Pudding
Hard Rolls	Spiced Peach	Orange and Cranberry	Butter Pecan Ice Cream
Corn Bread	Chutney	Head Lettuce	Date Marshmallow Roll

SUGGESTIONS FOR BEEF *(continued)*

MEAT	SOUP-APPETIZER	STARCHY FOOD	OTHER VEGETABLE
Beef Pot Pie	Tomato Juice	Potato Balls	Peas
	Grapefruit-Orange Cup	Potato Cubes	Diced Carrots and Onions
	Cream of Tomato Soup	Duchess Potatoes	Asparagus
Meat Loaf	Fruit Cocktail	Mashed Potatoes	Cauliflower Au Gratin
	Consommé	Creamed New Potatoes	Buttered Wax Beans
	Corn Soup	Au Gratin Potatoes	Asparagus Tips
Hamburgers	Broiled Grapefruit	French Fried Potatoes	Buttered Cabbage
	Scotch Broth	Hashed Browned Potatoes	Buttered Spinach
	Vegetable Juice	Escalloped Potatoes	Green Beans
Creamed Dried Beef	Minted Fruit Juice	Rice Ring	Buttered Broccoli
	Cantaloupe Quarters	Fried Noodles	Harvard Beets
	Cranberry Juice	Baked Potato	Asparagus
Frankfurters	Tomato Juice	Hot Potato Salad	Julienne Carrots
	Grapefruit	Macaroni and Cheese	Okra and Tomatoes
	Spinach Soup	Steamed Potatoes	Red Cabbage
Heart	Vegetable Juice	Rice Timbales	Fried Parsnips
	Asparagus Soup	Baked Potato	Peas and Carrots
	Lime-Pineapple Juice	Potato Puffs	Steamed Tomatoes
Kidneys	Clear Soup	Boiled Potatoes	Spinach
	Orange Sections	Rice Ring	Mushrooms
	Sauerkraut Juice	Mashed Potatoes	Brussels Sprouts
Liver	Tomato Bouillon	Creamed Potatoes	Fried Eggplant
	Broiled Grapefruit	Spanish Rice	French Fried Onions
	Split Pea Soup	Mashed Potatoes	Creamed Cabbage
Tongue	Tomato Juice	Boiled Potatoes	Spinach
	Noodle Soup	Potato Chips	Carrot and Cheese Soufflé
	Mushroom Soup	Escalloped Potatoes	Green Beans

SUGGESTIONS FOR BEEF *(continued)*

BREAD	ACCOMPANIMENT	SALAD	DESSERT
White Bread	Corn Relish	Fresh Vegetable	Apricot Whip
Biscuits	Spiced Peach	Cucumbers in Sour Cream	Spice Cake
Rye Bread	Currant Jelly	Head Lettuce	Fresh Pineapple
Soft Rolls	Worcestershire Sauce	Jellied Tomato	Chocolate Roll
Blueberry Muffins	Mustard Sauce	Pineapple-Carrot	Fruit
White Bread	Piccalilli	Apple-Grape	Chocolate Parfait
Soft Rolls	Tomato Sauce	Pickled Beets	Coconut Custard Pie
Sliced Bread	Celery-Olives	Cranberry Sauce	Date and Nut Pudding
Gingerbread	Spiced Peach	Celery	Raisin Pie
Cinnamon Rolls	Marmalade	Tomato Aspic	Cottage Pudding
Assorted Breads	Celery	Jellied Vegetable	Chocolate Pudding
Cheese Biscuits	Tart Jelly	Cole Slaw	Cherry Pie
Rye Bread	Barbecue Sauce	Jellied Fruit	Caramel Custard
Sliced Bread	Pickles-Olives	Celery-Nut	Rhubarb Pie
Hard Rolls	Celery	Stuffed Pear	Gingerbread
White Bread	Curry Sauce	Cucumber-Radish	Peach Pie
Corn Bread	Celery	Orange Mint	Chocolate Pudding
Soft Rolls	Pickled Onions	Mixed Green	Blackberry Cobbler
Toasted Rolls	Bacon	Tomato-Cucumber	Apple Pie
Hot Rolls	Creole Sauce	Jellied Vegetable	Ice Cream
Sliced Bread	Spanish Sauce	Rose Apple	Butterscotch Pudding
Sliced Bread	Fried Onions	Head Lettuce	Raspberry Sherbet
Soft Rolls	Bacon	Cole Slaw	Ice Cream
Corn Muffins	Chili Sauce	Pear with Cheese	Spice Cake
Sliced Bread	Raisin Sauce	Grated Carrot	Apricots
Raisin Bread	Spanish Sauce	Cranberry Jelly	Black Walnut Cake
Soft Rolls	Dill Pickles	Stuffed Tomato	Apple Strudel

SUGGESTIONS FOR VEAL

MEAT	SOUP-APPETIZER	STARCHY FOOD	OTHER VEGETABLE
Roast Leg of Veal	Fruit Cup Tomato Juice Seafood Cocktail	Mashed Potatoes Browned Potatoes Baked Potato	Buttered Spinach Parsley-Carrots Buttered Green Beans
Breaded Veal Cutlets	Consommé Gumbo Fruit Shrub	Creamed Potatoes Buttered Noodles Macaroni Au Gratin	Buttered Peas Stewed Tomatoes Asparagus Tips
Braised Veal Chops	Cream of Corn Soup Vegetable Juice Melon Balls	French Fried Potatoes Steamed Rice Browned Potatoes	Broccoli Buttered Beets Broiled Tomato
Roast Veal Shoulder	Chicken Bouillon Split Pea Soup Broiled Grapefruit	Mashed Potatoes Rice Creamed New Potatoes	Buttered Carrots Harvard Beets Brussels Sprouts
Stuffed Breast of Veal	Beef Broth Pineapple Juice Tomato Soup	Glazed Sweet Potatoes Corn on Cob Noodle Pudding	Buttered Green Beans Peas in Cream Asparagus
Veal Stew	Apricot Nectar Vegetable Juice Fruit Cup	Lima Beans Rice Dumplings	Carrots Peas Green Beans
Veal Pot Pie	Bean Soup Tomato Juice Chicken Noodle Soup	Potato Balls Mashed Potatoes Rice	Carrots and Peas Green Beans Stewed Tomatoes
Veal Loaf	Mushroom Soup Split Pea Soup Grapefruit	Stuffed Baked Potato Glazed Sweet Potatoes Macaroni and Cheese	Creamed Onions Fresh Peas Green Beans
Sweetbreads	Fruit Cup Consommé Chicken Soup	Creamed Potatoes Hashed Browned Potatoes Noodle Pudding	Asparagus Stewed Tomatoes Peas and Carrots
Brains	Grapefruit Juice Cream of Celery Soup Vegetable Juice	Browned Potatoes Potatoes Au Gratin French Fried Potatoes	Wax Beans Green Beans Braised Celery

Menu

SUGGESTIONS FOR VEAL

BREAD	ACCOMPANIMENT	SALAD	DESSERT
Soft Rolls	Brown Gravy	Fresh Vegetable	Apple Brown Betty
Muffins	Currant Jelly	Cucumbers in Cream	Peach Tarts
Sliced Bread	Spiced Peaches	Lettuce-Tomato	Pineapple Sherbet with Cake
Soft Rolls	Cranberry Sauce	Hearts of Celery	Cantaloupe
Rye Bread	Brown Gravy	Apple, Nut, White Grape	Ice Cream
Hard Rolls	Tomato Sauce	Cole Slaw	Peaches with Cookies
Gingerbread Muffins	Grape Jelly	Molded Vegetable	Chocolate Pudding
Rye Bread	Brown Gravy	Head Lettuce	Ice Cream
Soft Rolls	Pickle Relish	Asparagus	Blueberry Pie
White Bread	Brown Gravy	Head Lettuce	Orange Ice
Biscuits	Chili Sauce	Tossed Green	Fruit with Cookies
Whole Wheat Bread	Celery-Olives	Minted Pineapple	Date and Nut Pudding
Hard Rolls	Currant Jelly	Orange-Grapefruit	Ice Cream Roll
Hot Rolls	Brown Gravy	Mixed Green	Prune Whip
Rye Bread	Curry Sauce	Carrot-Raisin	Fruit Cup with Cookies
Pecan Muffins	Chili Sauce	Cole Slaw	Angel Food Cake
Soft Rolls	Plum Jelly	Waldorf	Custard
Hard Rolls	Dill Pickles	Cucumber	Tapioca
Biscuits	Crabapple Jelly	Pineapple	Gingerbread with Whipped Cream
Soft Rolls	Celery-Radishes	Molded Fruit	Chocolate Soufflé
Raisin Bread	Sweet Pickles	Celery-Apple	Spice Cake
Blueberry Muffins	Ketchup	Head Lettuce	Date Torte
Soft Rolls	Tomato Sauce	Spiced Beets	Peach Pie
Corn Bread	Pickle Relish	Tossed Green	Pumpkin Pie
Cheese Biscuits	Apple Jelly	Combination	Banana Cream Pie
Soft Rolls	Crisp Bacon	Cucumber-Onion	Ice Cream
Bacon Muffins	Mushrooms	Lettuce-Tomato	Apple Pie
Rye Bread	Mushroom Sauce	Head Lettuce	Strawberries
Hard Rolls	Broiled Peach Half	Molded Vegetable	Chocolate Cake
Drop Biscuits	Honey	Garden	Honey Dew Melon

Menu SUGGESTIONS FOR LAMB

MEAT	SOUP-APPETIZER	STARCHY FOOD	OTHER VEGETABLE
Roast Leg of Lamb	Antipasto Consommé Fruit Cup	Browned Potato Creamed Potatoes Au Gratin Potatoes	Fresh Peas Asparagus Spinach
Broiled Lamb Chops	Apricot Nectar Mushroom Soup Broiled Grapefruit	Creamed New Potatoes Hashed Browned Potatoes Spanish Rice	Green Beans with Celery Peas and Carrots Spinach
Lamb Shoulder	Pineapple Juice Asparagus Soup Jellied Consommé	Baked Potato Mashed Potatoes Fried Rice	Fried Eggplant Cauliflower Minted Carrots
Lamb Patties	Celery Soup Vegetable Juice Fruit Cup	Mashed Potatoes French Fries Home Fries	Green Beans Baby Beets Broccoli
Lamb Stew	Fresh Strawberry-Pineapple Tomato Juice Consommé	Cubed Potatoes Dumplings Rice	Peas and Carrots Peas with Celery Cabbage Au Gratin
Stuffed Breast of Lamb	Split Pea Soup Fruit Cup Vegetable Juice	Browned Potato Mashed Potatoes Candied Sweet Potatoes	Spinach Asparagus Broccoli

SUGGESTIONS FOR PORK

MEAT	SOUP-APPETIZER	STARCHY FOOD	OTHER VEGETABLE
Pork Sausage	Split Pea Soup Tomato Juice Grapefruit	Creamed Potatoes Mashed Potatoes Fried Noodles	Stewed Tomatoes Green Beans with Celery Sauerkraut
Baked Smoked Ham	Pineapple Shrub Cream of Spinach Soup Tomato Juice	Candied Yams Escalloped Potatoes Riced Potatoes	Fresh Peas Green Beans with Mushrooms Peas and Carrots

Menu SUGGESTIONS FOR LAMB

BREAD	ACCOMPANIMENT	SALAD	DESSERT
Soft Rolls	Mint Sauce	Jellied Vegetable	Ice Cream with Chocolate Brownies
Bread Sticks	Stewed Apricots	Head Lettuce	Gingerbread
Nut Muffins	Pineapple Mint Sherbet	Fresh Vegetable	Chocolate Chip Angel Food Cake
Hard Rolls	Caper Sauce	Lettuce-Tomato	Red Raspberry Tart
Sliced Bread	Pineapple Mint Sauce	Cucumber-Onion	Lemon Whip
Rye Bread	Currant Jelly	Tossed Green	Coconut Custard Pie
Cherry Muffins	Celery-Olives	Wilted Lettuce	Fruit-Cookies
Soft Rolls	Brown Gravy	Molded Pineapple-Carrot	Peppermint Stick Ice Cream
Corn Sticks	Spiced Pears	Tomato-Cucumber	Apple Tart
Rye Bread	Brown Gravy	Cranberry and Orange	Butterscotch Pudding
Bread Sticks	Peach Jam	Cole Slaw	Berry Pie
White Bread	Rhubarb Sauce	Head Lettuce	Spice Cake
Biscuits	Brown Gravy	Combination	Raisin Pie
Corn Sticks	Brown Butter	Celery-Apple	Peach Pie
Rye Bread	Sweet Pickles	Grated Carrot	Chocolate Ice Cream
Soft Rolls	Onion Sauce	Perfection	Apple Brown Betty
Biscuits	Brown Gravy	Head Lettuce	Chocolate Cake
Gingerbread Muffins	Celery-Olives	Garden	Fruit Compote

SUGGESTIONS FOR PORK

BREAD	ACCOMPANIMENT	SALAD	DESSERT
Corn Muffins	Apple Rings	Molded Fruit	Spice Cake
Bread Sticks	Brown Gravy	Cole Slaw	Apple Dumpling
Rye Bread	Carrot Sticks	Head Lettuce	Caramel Sundae
Biscuits	Cranberry Sauce	Pickled Beets	Blueberry Pie
Hot Rolls	Applesauce	Tossed Green	Orange Coconut Cake
Rye Bread	Raisin Sauce	Melon Ring with Fresh Fruit	Butter Pecan Ice Cream

SUGGESTIONS FOR PORK *(continue*

MEAT	SOUP-APPETIZER	STARCHY FOOD	OTHER VEGETABLE
Broiled Ham Slice	Melon Balls	Rice	Green Beans
	Pineapple Juice	Sweet Potato Puffs	Asparagus
	Crabmeat Cocktail	Lima Beans	Acorn Squash
Smoked Picnic Shoulder	Tomato Soup	Baked Potato	Buttered Peas
	Consommé	Glazed Sweet Potatoes	Cauliflower Au Grat
	Apricot Nectar	Rice Croquette	Swiss Chard
Canadian Bacon	Grapefruit	Creamed Potatoes	Asparagus
	Chicken Noodle Soup	Mashed Sweet Potatoes	Green Beans with Pimento
	Celery Soup	Parsley Lima Beans	Broccoli
Bacon	Split Pea Soup	Creamed Potatoes	Stewed Tomatoes
	Barley Soup	Hashed Browned Potatoes	Creamed Celery
	Tomato Juice	Spanish Rice	Green Beans
Roast Fresh Ham	Consommé	Browned Potatoes	Escalloped Tomatoe
	Broiled Grapefruit	Glazed Sweet Potatoes	Broccoli
	Fruit Cup	Mashed Potatoes	Acorn Squash
Roast Pork Tenderloin	Grapefruit	Mashed Potatoes	Carrots
	Split Pea Soup	Baked Sweet Potato	Asparagus
	Peach Nectar	Lima Beans	Broccoli
Crown Roast of Pork	Fresh Fruit Cocktail	Parsley Potatoes	Fried Eggplant
	Celery Soup	Browned Potatoes	Glazed Carrots
	Tomato Juice	Fried Noodles	Green Beans
Braised Pork Chops	Pickled Herring	Mashed Potatoes	Parsley Carrots
	Vegetable Juice	Spanish Rice	Green Beans
	Celery Soup	Browned Potatoes	Squash
Stuffed Pork Chops	Beef Broth	Fried Rice	Brussels Sprouts
	Shrimp Cocktail	Candied Sweet Potatoes	Fresh Peas
	Pineapple Juice	Wild Rice	Minted Carrots
Spareribs	Tomato Soup	Boiled Potatoes	Sauerkraut
	Grape Juice	Hashed Browned Potatoes	Broccoli
	Vegetable Soup	Hot Potato Salad	Green Beans

SUGGESTIONS FOR PORK *(continued)*

BREAD	ACCOMPANIMENT	SALAD	DESSERT
Corn Sticks	Milk Gravy	Molded Cranberry	Cottage Pudding with Caramel Sauce
Biscuits	Cranberry Sauce	Head Lettuce	Tapioca Cream
Hard Rolls	Mustard Sauce	Stuffed Peach	Gingerbread
Rye Bread	Apricot Sauce	Celery-Nut	Butterscotch Sundae
Soft Rolls	Spiced Crab Apple	Spinach-Lettuce	Cherry Pie
Raisin Bread	Pineapple Sherbet	Head Lettuce	Chocolate Cake
Biscuits	Honey	Cottage Cheese with Chives	Coconut Custard Pie
Cherry Muffins	Apple Rings	Mixed Vegetable	Cottage Pudding with Chocolate Sauce
Soft Rolls	Mustard Sauce	Tomato-Cucumber	Peach Dumpling
Toasted Rolls	Plum Jam	Cole Slaw	Apricots with Brownies
Hard Rolls	Currant Jelly	Cucumber	Dutch Apple Cake
Soft Rolls	Celery-Olives	Head Lettuce	Cheese Cake
Hard Rolls	Applesauce	Head Lettuce	Pineapple Sherbet
Soft Rolls	Celery-Olives	Cabbage-Carrot	Lemon Pie
Biscuits	Peach Jam	Spiced Beet	Apple Cobbler
Corn Bread	Honey	Cole Slaw	Lemon Sherbet
Bacon Muffins	Broiled Peach Half	Tossed Green	Raisin Bread Pudding
Sally Lunn Squares	Beet Relish	Raisin-Carrot	Spice Cake
Soft Rolls	Celery Hearts	Asparagus Spears	Date Nut Torte
Hard Rolls	Prune Stuffing	Jellied Fruit	Ice Cream
Cherry Muffins	Cranberry Sauce	Sliced Tomato	Coconut Cream Pie
French Bread	Brown Gravy	Cole Slaw	Baked Apple
Blueberry Muffins	Stuffed Celery	Grapefruit-Orange	Gingerbread with Whipped Cream
Whole Wheat Bread	Spiced Peach	Molded Vegetable	Canned Pears with Spice Cookies
Salt Rye Sticks	Chili Sauce	Head Lettuce	Peach Pie
Corn Bread	Celery Hearts	Waldorf	Lemon Snow
Soft Rolls	Apple Rings	Tossed Green	Strawberry Sundae
Pumpernickel	Ketchup	Jellied Vegetable	Applesauce Cake
Hard Rolls	Green Pepper Relish	Cole Slaw	Lemon Tarts
Soft Rolls	Spiced Crab Apple	Tomato	Butterscotch Pudding

BEEF RECIPES

Temperature-Time Chart For Roast Beef

325° F. Oven Temperature

Use rack in uncovered roaster.
Add no water.
Do not baste.

Cut	Approximate Minutes Per Pound 3-5 Pounds	Approximate Minutes Per Pound 5-8 Pounds	Meat Thermometer Reading When Roast Is Done
Rolled Rib			
Weight after boning, rolling			
Rare	31–36	27–32	140° F.
Medium	36–40	32–36	160° F.
Well Done	40–45	38–43	170° F.
Standing Rib			
Rare	21–26	17–22	140° F.
Medium	26–30	22–26	160° F.
Well Done	30–35	28–33	170° F.

Note:
If doing a 9-10 pound standing rib roast, use oven temperature of 325° F.
Rare: 20 minutes per pound or 140 F. thermometer reading.
Medium: 25 minutes per pound or 160 F. thermometer reading.

BEEF Recipes

ROAST BEEF

Standing Rib or Rolled Rib

1. Wipe meat with damp cloth to remove any small loose pieces of bone.
2. Rub meat on all sides with the cut side of a clove of garlic.
3. Sprinkle with salt, pepper if desired, but never flour it. It makes little difference if meat is salted before or after cooking because salt only penetrates to about ½ inch depth.
4. Place on rack in open roasting pan with fat side up.
5. Do not cover; add no water; do not baste during roasting period.
6. If using a meat thermometer insert into center of thickest meaty part of roast, being certain bulb does not rest on bone, fat or gristle.
7. Roast according to chart.

ROAST FILLET OF BEEF

Beef Tenderloin

2–3½ pounds beef tenderloin
1½ teaspoons salt
⅛ teaspoon pepper
¼ pound bacon or salt pork, sliced

1. Place meat on rack in open roasting pan.
2. Sprinkle with salt, pepper; lay bacon or salt pork strips over meat.
3. Roast in moderate oven 325° F.
   Rare: 22 minutes per pound
   Medium: 25 minutes per pound
4. Because of lack of fat through this cut of meat, it is not advisable to roast it to a well done stage.
5. Do not add water; do not cover; do not baste during roasting period.
6. Six servings.

POT ROAST OF BEEF

3–4 pounds beef, rump, chuck, shoulder
2 teaspoons salt
¼ teaspoon pepper
1 onion, peeled, sliced

1. Heat Dutch Oven or heavy fry pan; add meat; brown thoroughly on all sides.
2. Sprinkle with salt, pepper.
3. Place onion slices on top.
4. Cover; cook over low heat 4–4½ hours or until meat is tender.
5. If desired, potatoes, carrots may be added during last hour of cooking.
6. Thicken gravy.
7. Six servings.

BEEF Recipes

Broiling Time Table For Steaks

Turn meat after broiling ½ the time

CUT	THICKNESS	TOTAL APPROXIMATE TIME		
		Rare	*Medium*	*Well Done*
Beef				
Club Steak	1 inch	8–10 minutes	11–13 minutes	13–15 minutes
	1 ½ inches	16–18 minutes	19–21 minutes	21–25 minutes
Filet Mignon (or tenderloin)	1 inch	5– 6 minutes	7– 8 minutes	8–10 minutes
	1 ½ inches	8–10 minutes	11–13 minutes	13–15 minutes
	2 inches	11–13 minutes	15–17 minutes	17–19 minutes
Hamburgers	1 ½ inches		8–10 minutes	10–12 minutes
Porterhouse Steak	1 inch	8–10 minutes	11–13 minutes	13–15 minutes
	1 ½ inches	16–18 minutes	19–21 minutes	21–23 minutes
	2 inches	27–30 minutes	34–36 minutes	36–40 minutes
Rib Steak	1 inch	8–10 minutes	11–13 minutes	13–15 minutes
Sirloin Steak	1 inch	10–12 minutes	12–14 minutes	14–16 minutes
	1 ½ inches	18–20 minutes	20–24 minutes	24–26 minutes
	2 inches	34–36 minutes	36–40 minutes	40–42 minutes
T-Bone Steak	1 inch	8–10 minutes	11–13 minutes	13–15 minutes
	1 ½ inches	16–18 minutes	19–21 minutes	21–23 minutes
	2 inches	27–30 minutes	34–36 minutes	36–38 minutes

BROILED STEAK

1. Turn oven regulator to "broil" or to highest degree of setting. If no regulator, turn heat on full.

2. Preheat broiler 10 minutes or as directed by range manufacturer.

3. Trim surplus fat from meat; if meat is very lean like filet mignon, brush surface with fat.

4. Slash fat edge of meat at 2 inch intervals to prevent curling.

5. If desired, steak may be rubbed with cut side of clove of garlic or spread thinly with prepared mustard.

6. Grease broiler rack; add steak.

7. Place broiler pan at least 1½ inches below heat. The thicker the steak, the greater the distance.

8. Broil about ½ the approximate time; season; turn.

9. Broil second side remaining time; season; serve at once.

BEEF Recipes

STUFFED STEAK ROAST

2 pound slice round steak
1 teaspoon salt
¼ teaspoon pepper
2 cups dry bread crumbs
3 tablespoons grated onion
1 teaspoon sage
⅓ cup milk
2 tablespoons ketchup
1 egg, beaten

1. Wipe steak with damp cloth; season with salt, pepper.
2. Combine remaining ingredients.
3. Spread stuffing on steak; roll as jelly roll; tie with string.
4. Place roll on rack in open roaster; roast 45 minutes in moderate oven 350° F.
5. Six servings.

PANBROILED STEAK

1. Place aluminum fry pan over medium high heat; put a small piece of white paper in pan.
2. When paper turns a golden brown, drop steak in pan.
3. Allow meat to brown thoroughly on one side. When the cold meat hits the hot pan, it will stick but as it browns it will loosen itself.
4. Turn meat to brown second side; season; serve.
5. Heat may be reduced to medium after meat has been added. However, if juices start to cook out of meat, increase heat slightly.

SWISS STEAK

1½ pounds round steak, 1½ inches thick
2 tablespoons flour
1 teaspoon salt
⅛ teaspoon pepper
2 tablespoons melted fat
1 cup hot water
3 large onions, peeled, sliced

1. Trim excess fat from meat; cut into serving size pieces.
2. Combine flour, salt, pepper.
3. Place meat on breadboard; sprinkle with half of flour mixture; pound it into meat using rim of saucer.
4. Turn meat; pound remaining flour into second side.
5. Melt fat in heavy fry pan or Dutch Oven.
6. Brown meat on both sides over medium heat.
7. Add water, onions; cover; cook over low heat 1½–2 hours or until meat is tender.
8. More water may be added if necessary during cooking.
9. Four servings.

Variations

1. Use 1½ cups canned tomatoes instead of water.
2. Substitute tomato sauce or vegetable juice for all or part of water.
3. Add 2 tablespoons ketchup, ½ teaspoon prepared mustard to water.
4. Add 1 green pepper, seeded and cut into thin rings.

BEEF Recipes

DEVON STEAKS

- 3 pounds round steak, cut 1 inch thick
- 1 clove garlic, cut in half
- ½ cup flour
- 2½ teaspoons salt
- 1 tablespoon paprika
- 1 cup sliced onion
- 1 cup sliced mushrooms
- ¼ cup fat
- ½ cup hot water
- 1 cup sour cream

1. Cut meat into 8 serving pieces.
2. Rub each piece with cut side of garlic.
3. Mix flour, salt, paprika together; pound into meat.
4. Brown onions, mushrooms in fat in heavy fry pan; add meat; brown on both sides.
5. Add water; cover; cook over low heat 40–45 minutes or until meat is tender; add more water if necessary.
6. Pour sour cream over meat; re-cover; simmer 10 minutes longer.
7. Eight servings.

EVERYDAY HAMBURGERS

- 1½ pounds round steak, ground
- ⅓ cup slightly crushed corn flakes
- 1½ teaspoons salt
- ¼ teaspoon pepper
- 3 tablespoons grated onion

1. Combine all ingredients; shape into 8 patties.
2. Heat fry pan; add patties; brown on both sides.
3. Four servings.

BEEF STROGANOFF

- 3 tablespoons butter
- ½ pound fresh mushrooms or 2 four ounce cans
- 1 large onion, cut into ½ inch slices
- 1½–2 pounds flank steak
- 1 tablespoon bottled horseradish
- ½ cup water
- 1 teaspoon thick condiment sauce
- 1¼ teaspoons salt
- ⅛ teaspoon pepper
- 1 cup sour cream

1. Melt butter in fry pan; sauté mushrooms, onion slices 5 minutes; remove from fat.
2. Trim fat from steak; mince fat; add to butter in fry pan.
3. Remove tough, fibrous skin from steak.
4. Slice meat across grain into 1 inch strips; roll in flour; brown on all sides in butter.
5. Place onion mushroom mixture on top of meat; add horseradish, water, condiment sauce, salt, pepper.
6. Cover; cook over low heat 2 hours or until meat is tender.
7. Just before serving, add sour cream; thicken gravy if desired.
8. Six servings.

BEEF Recipes

BEEF STEW

- 1¾ pounds beef, 1½ inches thick, chuck or round
- ⅓ cup flour
- ¼ teaspoon pepper
- ½ teaspoon salt
- 3 tablespoons fat or drippings
- ¼ cup diced onion
- 1 minced clove of garlic
- 2¾ cups boiling water
- 1 cup canned tomatoes
- ½ teaspoon salt
- ½ teaspoon Worcestershire Sauce
- 3–4 medium potatoes, pared, quartered
- 12 small white onions, peeled
- 12 carrots, peeled, cut into 2-inch pieces
- 1 cup frozen peas (½ pkg.)

1. Trim excess fat from meat; cut into 1½ inch cubes.
2. Combine flour, pepper, salt in paper bag; add meat; shake until pieces are coated.
3. Melt fat in Dutch Oven; add meat; brown on all sides.
4. Add diced onion, garlic, boiling water, canned tomatoes, salt, Worcestershire Sauce.
5. Cover; reduce heat to low; simmer 2 hours or until meat is tender.
6. Add potatoes, onions, carrots; cook 20 minutes.
7. Add peas; cook 15 minutes longer.
8. Serves four.

Variations

1. Potatoes may be mashed and served as a border around stew; sprinkle potatoes with parsley.
2. Drop dumplings may be added when peas are put in to cook.
3. Stew may be served over cooked noodles, in which case omit potatoes.
4. Place stew in casserole; top with baking powder biscuits or flaky pastry; bake 20–25 minutes in hot oven 450° F.

HUNGARIAN GOULASH

With Noodles

- 1 pound beef, cut into cubes
- 2 medium onions, minced
- ¼ teaspoon dry mustard
- 1¼ teaspoons paprika
- 2 tablespoons brown sugar
- 1¼ teaspoons salt
- 3 tablespoons Worcestershire Sauce
- ¾ teaspoon cider vinegar
- 6 tablespoons ketchup
- 1½ cups water
- 3 tablespoons flour
- 1 6-ounce package noodles

1. Brown meat on all sides in heavy fry pan or Dutch Oven; add onion.
2. Combine mustard, paprika, brown sugar, salt.
3. Combine Worcestershire Sauce, vinegar, ketchup; add to mustard mixture; add to meat; add 1 cup of the water; stir; cover.
4. Cook over low heat 2½ hours or until meat is very tender.
5. Blend flour with remaining ½ cup water; add to meat mixture; stir until thickened.
6. Boil noodles in salted water until tender; drain.
7. Serve meat mixture over noodles.
8. Eight servings.

BEEF Recipes

SAUERBRATEN

3 pounds beef, round or shoulder
½ cup vinegar
½ cup water
1 small onion, thinly sliced
2 bay leaves
3 whole cloves
2 teaspoons salt
⅛ teaspoon pepper
4 tablespoons fat
1 cup water

1. Place meat in bowl.
2. Combine vinegar, water, onion, bay leaves, cloves, salt, pepper; blend.
3. Pour over meat; let stand 18–24 hours.
4. Melt fat in heavy fry pan or Dutch Oven.
5. Add meat; brown thoroughly on both sides.
6. Add water to liquid in which meat was soaked; pour over meat.
7. Cover; simmer over low heat 3 hours or until meat is tender.
8. Remove meat; make gravy from juices in pan.
9. Six servings.

PEPPER STEAK

2 tablespoons fat
1 pound round or flank steak
1 teaspoon salt
⅛ teaspoon pepper
2 tablespoons minced onion
1 clove garlic, minced
2 green peppers, diced
1 cup canned beef bouillon
1 cup drained canned tomatoes or 3 tomatoes, quartered
1½ tablespoons cornstarch
2 teaspoons soy sauce
¼ cup water

1. Melt fat in fry pan.
2. Cut meat into 1 inch strips; sprinkle with salt, pepper.
3. Place meat, onion, garlic in fry pan; brown.
4. Add peppers, bouillon; cover; cook 30 minutes.
5. Add tomatoes; simmer 5 minutes.
6. Combine cornstarch, soy sauce, water; add to meat mixture; cook 5 minutes, stirring constantly.
7. Four servings.

BRAISED SHORT RIBS OF BEEF

2 pounds beef short ribs, cut into 3 inch pieces
1 clove garlic, peeled, cut in half
2 tablespoons flour
2 teaspoons salt
½ teaspoon pepper
2 tablespoons fat
1½ cups boiling water
1 large onion, sliced

1. Lightly rub short ribs with cut side of garlic.
2. Combine flour, salt, pepper.
3. Coat meat with flour mixture.
4. Melt fat in heavy fry pan; add meat; brown on all sides.
5. Add water, sliced onions.
6. Cover; cook over low heat 2 hours or until meat is loosened from bones.
7. Four servings.

BEEF Recipes

Beef Budget Stretchers

MEAT LOAF

2 eggs, beaten
1½ pounds ground beef
½ pound ground pork
2 cups soft bread crumbs
¾ cup minced onion
¼ cup minced green pepper
2 tablespoons bottled horseradish
1 tablespoon salt
¼ cup milk
¼ cup ketchup
1 teaspoon dry mustard

1. Add eggs to meat; blend lightly with fork.
2. Add remaining ingredients; mix thoroughly but do not stir more than necessary as it tends to toughen loaf.
3. Shape into an oval loaf; place in shallow pan.
4. Bake 1 hour in hot oven 400° F.
5. Six servings.

Variations

1. Pack mixture into 9″ x 5″ x 3″ loaf pan; bake as above. To remove from pan, drain off liquid; unmold on cake rack; then turn right side up on heated platter.
2. Spread top with ½ cup ketchup before baking.
3. Place ½ of meat mixture in loaf pan; make three depressions using a tablespoon; place a shelled hard cooked egg in each depression; add remaining meat.
4. Pack mixture into ring mold. To serve, fill center with mashed potatoes.

STUFFED MEAT LOAF

Loaf

1½ pounds ground beef
½ pound ground pork
1 tablespoon minced onion
2 tablespoons horseradish
1 egg, beaten slightly
1 teaspoon salt
⅛ teaspoon pepper

1. Combine all ingredients; blend.
2. Pat mixture into bottom and around sides of 9″ x 5″ x 3″ loaf pan to thickness of ¾ inch.

Stuffing

4 cups mashed potatoes
½ teaspoon salt
1 teaspoon paprika
2 tablespoons minced pimento
2 tablespoons minced green pepper
2 egg yolks, well beaten
¼ cup milk

1. Combine ingredients in order given; blend.
2. Pack into meat lined pan.
3. Score top with tines of a fork.
4. Bake 1 hour in moderately hot oven 375° F.
5. Eight servings.

Variations

1. ½ cup chopped peanuts may be added to potatoes.
2. Grate yellow cheese over potatoes before baking.

BEEF Recipes

BEEFBURGER PIE

With Cheese Puff

2 tablespoons fat
2 tablespoons chopped onion
¾ pound ground beef
1 teaspoon salt
⅛ teaspoon pepper
2 tablespoons flour
2 cups tomatoes
½ teaspoon Worcestershire Sauce
1 cup diced cooked carrots
1 cup cooked green beans

Cheese Puff

1 cup sifted all purpose flour
1½ teaspoons baking powder
½ teaspoon dry mustard
½ teaspoon salt
2 tablespoons shortening
¼ cup grated sharp cheese
½ cup milk

1. Melt fat in fry pan; add onion, meat; brown well.
2. Add salt, pepper, flour; mix.
3. Add tomatoes, Worcestershire Sauce; cook until slightly thickened.
4. Add cooked carrots, green beans.
5. Pour into greased casserole or 8″ x 8″ x 2″ cake pan.
6. To make topping:
   a. Sift flour, baking powder, mustard, salt together; cut in shortening; add cheese, milk; blend to a soft dough.
   b. Pour topping over meat mixture; spread evenly.
   c. Bake 20–25 minutes in moderate oven 350° F.
7. Six servings.

HAMBURGER PATTIES

With Roquefort Spread

1 pound ground beef
2 tablespoons fat
½ cup hot water
¼ cup Roquefort cheese, crumbled
3 tablespoons soft butter
1 tablespoon prepared mustard
Few drops Worcestershire Sauce
Salt, pepper

1. Shape meat into eight thin patties; brown lightly on both sides in hot fat in heavy fry pan.
2. Add water; cover; cook over low heat 10 minutes.
3. Combine cheese, butter, mustard, Worcestershire Sauce, salt, pepper.
4. Spread over patties; cover; cook 5 minutes longer.
5. Four servings.

BEEF Recipes

CHILI CON CARNE

1 tablespoon butter
1 pound ground beef
½ cup diced onion
1 No. 2 can red kidney beans
2 cups tomato soup
1 teaspoon salt
¼ teaspoon chili powder

1. Melt butter in heavy fry pan; add meat, onion; cook until brown; stir frequently.
2. Add remaining ingredients; stir; cover.
3. Cook over low heat 20–25 minutes; stir occasionally.
4. Four servings.

Note: additional chili powder may be added.

BEEF ROLI POLI

Part One:

3 tablespoons fat
1 pound beef, ground or
2 cups ground leftover beef
1 cup chopped mushrooms
1 medium onion, minced
2 eggs, beaten
1½ teaspoons salt
⅛ teaspoon pepper
1 tablespoon minced parsley

1. Melt fat in fry pan; add meat, mushrooms, onions; cook until brown, stirring occasionally.
2. Add eggs, salt, pepper, parsley; mix well; set aside to cool.

Part Two:

3 cups sifted all purpose flour
4½ teaspoons baking powder
1 teaspoon salt
2 tablespoons sugar
½ cup shortening
1 cup milk

1. Sift dry ingredients together; cut in shortening; add milk to make a soft dough.
2. Roll on lightly floured board to ½ inch thickness.
3. Spread with meat mixture; roll up as for jelly roll.
4. Cut into 1 inch slices; place in shallow baking pan; brush with butter.
5. Bake 20–25 minutes in hot oven, 425° F.
6. Serve with a sauce made by adding 1 cup leftover cooked vegetables to 3 cups mushroom soup or to equal amount of gravy.
7. Eight servings.

BEEF Recipes

BEEF PATTIES

With Tomato Cheese Topping

- 1½ pounds ground beef
- ½ cup soft bread crumbs
- ¾ teaspoon salt
- ⅛ teaspoon pepper
- 1 egg, beaten
- 1½ tablespoons prepared mustard
- 6 slices onion
- 6 slices American cheese ¼ inch thick
- ¾ cup condensed tomato soup

1. Combine meat, crumbs, salt, pepper, egg; shape into 6 patties; place in shallow baking pan.

2. Spread patties with mustard; place one slice onion, cheese on each.

3. Pour tomato soup over top.

4. Bake 35–40 minutes in moderate oven 400° F.

5. Six servings.

BEEF PATTIES with Onion Sauce

- 1 pound ground beef
- 1 teaspoon salt
- ¼ teaspoon pepper
- ¼ cup butter or margarine
- 3 cups sliced, peeled onions
- 2 cups boiling water
- 1 teaspoon bottled thick condiment sauce
- ¼ cup cold water
- 2 tablespoons cornstarch

1. Combine meat, salt, pepper; shape into 4 patties.

2. Panbroil patties on both sides until brown; remove from pan.

3. Melt butter; add onions; cook until deep brown.

4. Add boiling water, condiment sauce; stir.

5. Combine cold water, cornstarch; stir into sauce; cook, stirring constantly until clear and thickened; add salt, pepper to taste.

6. Place patties in sauce; cover; reduce heat to simmer; cook 5 minutes.

7. Four servings.

TALLARENE

- 3 tablespoons fat
- 1 medium onion, minced
- 1 pound beef, ground
- 1½ cups tomato soup
- 1 cup cold water
- 1 teaspoon salt
- 2 cups uncooked broad noodles
- 2 cups whole grain corn
- 1 cup chopped ripe olives
- 1 cup grated sharp cheese

1. Melt fat in heavy fry pan or Dutch Oven.

2. Add onion, ground beef; cook until browned.

3. Add soup, water, salt, noodles, corn, olives; mix thoroughly.

4. Sprinkle cheese over top; cover; cook over low heat 15-20 minutes or until noodles are tender.

5. Eight servings.

BEEF Recipes

BARBECUED MEAT PATTIES

¾ pound ground beef
¼ pound ground pork
1½ cups coarsely grated raw potatoes
½ cup grated onion
¼ cup chopped green pepper
2 teaspoons salt
¼ teaspoon pepper
1 tablespoon granulated sugar
2 tablespoons fat
⅓ cup ketchup
¼ teaspoon celery salt
⅛ teaspoon Tabasco

1. Combine beef, pork, potatoes, onion, green pepper, salt, pepper, sugar; mix well.
2. Shape into 12 patties, about 2 inches diameter.
3. Brown patties on both sides in hot fat in heavy fry pan.
4. Combine ketchup, celery salt, Tabasco; pour over meat; cover; reduce heat to low; cook 10-15 minutes longer.
5. Six servings.

DOUBLE DECKER HAMBURGERS

1½ pounds ground round steak
¾ cup cold water
1 teaspoon salt
½ teaspoon pepper
¼ cup ketchup
3 tablespoons soft butter or margarine
4 large stuffed olives, sliced
1 medium onion, sliced, broken into rings

1. Combine meat, water, salt, pepper; shape into 8 flat patties.
2. Brown in fry pan.
3. Place 4 patties in shallow baking pan; spread with ketchup, sliced olives.
4. Top with remaining 4 patties.
5. Spread with butter; insert toothpicks through center of each patty; hang onion rings over toothpicks.
6. Bake 40-45 minutes in moderate oven 375° F.

PORCUPINE BEEF BALLS

½ cup uncooked rice
1 pound beef, ground
1½ teaspoons salt
¼ teaspoon pepper
2 tablespoons minced onion
2 tablespoons fat
1 cup condensed tomato soup
1 cup hot water

1. Combine rice, beef, salt, pepper, onion; mix; shape into 12 balls.
2. Brown balls in fat in heavy fry pan; add tomato soup, water.
3. Cover; cook 1½ hours over low heat until rice is tender.
4. Six servings.

BEEF Recipes

GREEN PEPPER STEAK

A La Chinese

- 1 tablespoon soy sauce
- 1 clove garlic
- ¼ cup salad oil
- 1 pound round steak cut into 1 inch cubes
- 1 green pepper, cut into 1 inch cubes
- 1 large onion, coarsely chopped
- ½ cup diced celery
- 1 teaspoon cornstarch
- ¼ cup water
- 2 tomatoes, cut into eighths

1. Mix soy sauce, garlic, salad oil together; pour over steak; let stand one hour.
2. Pour into fry pan; allow meat to brown thoroughly on all sides.
3. Add pepper, onion, celery; cover; cook 5–10 minutes over low heat or until vegetables are tender.
4. Stir in cornstarch dissolved in water, stir until thickened; add tomatoes; cover; cook 5–10 minutes longer or until meat is tender; serve over boiled rice.
5. Four servings.

SPAGHETTI WITH MEAT SAUCE

- 4 tablespoons butter or olive oil
- 1 cup chopped onion
- 2 cloves garlic, finely minced
- 1 cup mushrooms, chopped
- 1 pound ground beef
- ½ cup chopped celery
- 3 tablespoons flour
- ½ cup beef stock or one bouillon cube dissolved in ½ cup hot water
- ¼ cup sour red wine
- ½ can tomato paste
- 1 No. 2 can tomatoes
- Salt, pepper
- 1 tablespoon parsley
- 1 package fine spaghetti
- Parmesan cheese

1. Melt butter in heavy fry pan or Dutch Oven.
2. Sauté onion, garlic 5 minutes.
3. Add mushrooms, meat; brown lightly.
4. Add celery, flour, stock, wine, tomato paste, tomatoes, salt, pepper, parsley; mix thoroughly.
5. Cover; cook over very low heat 30–40 minutes; more wine and stock may be added if sauce gets too thick.
6. Boil spaghetti in salted water until tender; drain; rinse.
7. Pile spaghetti on plates; top with sauce; serve with Parmesan cheese.
8. Four servings.

BEEF Recipes

SLOPPY JOES

¼ cup sliced onions
½ cup diced green pepper
2 tablespoons fat
2 medium tomatoes, peeled
¾ cup diced mushrooms
½ pound ground beef
1 cup tomato juice
¼ teaspoon paprika
¼ teaspoon pepper
¾ teaspoon salt

1. Sauté onion, green pepper in fat in heavy fry pan until lightly browned.

2. Cut tomatoes into eighths; add.

3. Add mushrooms, beef, tomato juice, paprika, pepper, salt.

4. Cover; cook over low heat 15–20 minutes.

5. Thicken juice if desired; serve over split toasted buns.

BARBECUED HAMBURGERS NO. 1

1½ pounds ground beef
⅓ cup corn flakes, crushed slightly
1½ teaspoons salt
¼ teaspoon pepper
3 tablespoons grated onion
¼ cup ketchup
⅛ teaspoon Tabasco Sauce
⅛ teaspoon chili powder
½ cup hot water

1. Combine beef, corn flakes, salt, pepper, onion; shape into patties.

2. Brown patties on both sides in heavy fry pan.

3. Combine ketchup, Tabasco Sauce, chili powder, water; pour over patties.

4. Cover; cook over low heat 20–25 minutes.

5. Six servings.

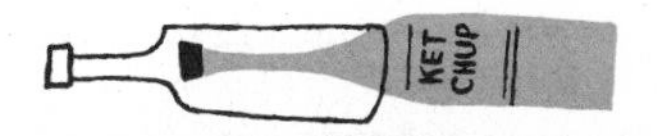

BARBECUED HAMBURGERS NO. 2

1½ pounds ground beef
⅓ cup corn flakes, crushed slightly
1½ teaspoons salt
¼ teaspoon pepper
3 tablespoons grated onion
2 tablespoons fat
1 large onion, diced
1 cup tomatoes
1 cup diced celery
1 cup diced green pepper
1 cup ketchup
2 tablespoons brown sugar
¼ teaspoon Tabasco Sauce
½ tablespoon dry mustard
2 cups beef stock
Salt
Pepper

1. Combine meat, corn flakes, salt, pepper and the 3 tablespoons onion; shape into patties.

2. Melt fat in Dutch Oven; add patties; brown on both sides; remove from pan.

3. Add onion; brown lightly.

4. Add remaining ingredients; stir; cover; cook 15 minutes.

5. Add patties; cook 45 minutes longer.

6. Six servings.

BEEF Recipes

Leftover Dishes

ROAST BEEF HASH

2 cups chopped leftover roast beef
2-3 cups chopped cooked potatoes
6 tablespoons minced onion
Salt, pepper
⅓ cup light cream or milk
2 tablespoons fat

1. Chop meat, potatoes, separately; pieces should be a little smaller than ¼ inch cubes.
2. Add onion, seasoning, cream; toss together lightly.
3. Melt fat in heavy fry pan or in both sides of omelet pan.
4. Put hash into pan; spread evenly.
5. Cook uncovered over low heat, without stirring until underside is lightly browned, about 30–35 minutes. Check browning by lifting edge with spatula; if browning too rapidly reduce heat.
6. Run spatula around sides of pan to loosen hash.
7. If using the omelet pan, close to put the 2 halves together, then turn onto heated platter.
8. If using fry pan, take handle in left hand; make a cut through center of hash at right angle to handle. Tip handle up and with aid of spatula, fold upper half over lower half.
9. Hold edge of pan close to far edge of platter; slowly tip the two together until hash rolls onto platter.
10. Four servings.

BEEF POT PIE

½ cup minced onion
½ cup finely diced celery
¾ cup sliced mushrooms
2 tablespoons fat
2 tablespoons flour
2 cups cubed leftover beef
1 cup diced cooked potatoes
1 cup sliced cooked carrots
2 tablespoons chopped parsley
1 tablespoon Worcestershire Sauce
1 teaspoon salt
⅛ teaspoon pepper
1 cup leftover gravy
Flaky pastry

1. Cook onion, celery, mushrooms in fat over low heat about 10 minutes or until tender; stir in flour.
2. Add remaining ingredients; blend; cover; simmer 10 minutes.
3. Pour into greased casserole or 8″ x 8″ x 2″ cake pan.
4. Roll pastry ⅛ inch thick; make several gashes in center.
5. Place on top of meat-vegetable mixture; brush with slightly beaten egg white or ice water.
6. Bake 20 minutes in hot oven 450° F.
7. Six servings.

BEEF Recipes

SWEET AND SOUR MEAT SLICES

1 pound leftover beef or pork roast
2 tablespoons flour
2 tablespoons fat
2 teaspoons drained horseradish
2 teaspoons prepared mustard
¼ cup ketchup
1 teaspoon grated onion
2 teaspoons vinegar
¼ teaspoon salt
⅛ teaspoon pepper
½ cup sweet pickle relish
½ cup hot water

1. Cut meat into ¼ inch slices; roll in flour; brown lightly in fat in heavy fry pan.

2. Combine remaining ingredients; pour over meat.

3. Cover; cook over low heat 15–20 minutes.

4. Four servings.

BAKED BEEF HASH

2 cups ground leftover beef
2–3 cups finely diced cooked potatoes
6 tablespoons minced onion
Salt, pepper
1 cup leftover gravy
2 cups buttered bread crumbs

1. Combine meat, potatoes, onion, seasoning, gravy; blend thoroughly.

2. Pour into greased casserole or 8″ x 8″ x 2″ cake pan.

3. Spread crumbs over top.

4. Bake 20–25 minutes in moderate oven 350° F.

5. Four servings.

DRIED BEEF

FRIZZLED DRIED BEEF

1. Sauté dried beef in butter or margarine until edges curl and beef is browned slightly.

2. Serve as is or with scrambled eggs.

CREAMED CHIP BEEF

2½ tablespoons butter
2½ tablespoons flour
2½ cups milk
⅛ teaspoon pepper
¼ pound chipped dried beef
4 hard cooked eggs, peeled

1. Melt butter over boiling water in top of double boiler.

2. Add flour, milk; stir until sauce is smooth; add pepper.

3. Tear dried beef into small pieces; place in strainer; let hot water run over it; drain; add to sauce.

4. Cut eggs in eighths; add.

5. Blend together lightly; serve on toast.

6. Four servings.

BEEF Recipes

Wieners

SNOW CAPS

- 4 wieners
- 4 cups mashed potatoes
- 1 tablespoon chopped green onions
- ½ cup grated American cheese

1. Split wieners lengthwise; place in shallow pan.
2. Combine mashed potatoes, green onions; pile on top of wieners.
3. Sprinkle cheese over potatoes.
4. Bake 20–25 minutes in moderate oven 400° F.
5. Sprinkle with paprika; serve.
6. Four servings.

BOILED WIENERS

1. Drop wieners into boiling water; cover; simmer 5 minutes.

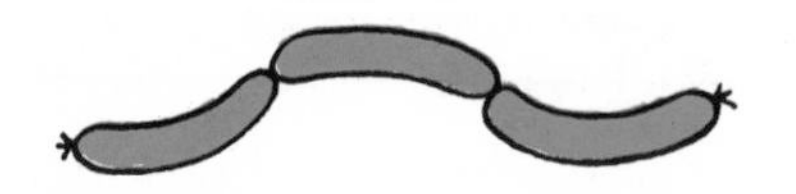

BROILED STUFFED WIENERS

With Beans

- 4 wieners
- 1 tablespoon prepared mustard
- 2 dill pickles, sliced lengthwise
- 2 4"x4" pieces sharp cheese, cut into halves
- 4 strips bacon
- 2 cans baked beans

1. Split wieners lengthwise; spread with mustard.
2. Insert one slice pickle, one slice cheese into each wiener.
3. Wrap one strip bacon around each wiener; fasten with toothpicks.
4. Broil until brown on all sides.
5. Heat beans; add juices in bottom of broiler pan to beans.
6. Pile beans in center of platter; surround with wieners.
7. Four servings.

20th CENTURY WIENERS

- 3 tomatoes, sliced thin
- 2 medium onions, peeled, sliced
- 6 wieners, cut into 1 inch pieces
- ⅛ teaspoon basil
- ⅓ cup shredded sharp cheese

1. Alternate tomatoes, onions, wieners in fry pan; sprinkle basil on top.
2. Cover; cook over low heat 30 minutes.
3. Sprinkle cheese over top just before serving.
4. Four servings.

BEEF Recipes

Corned Beef

CORNED BEEF AND CABBAGE

1. Wash; quarter medium head cabbage; remove most of core.

2. About 20 minutes before corned beef is done, place cabbage on top of meat.

3. Cover; boil until cabbage is just tender—no longer.

CORNED BEEF

4-5 pounds mild cure brisket of beef
3 sliced onions
3 whole cloves
6 peppercorns
1 bay leaf
1 clove garlic, peeled, quartered
1 stalk celery
1 peeled carrot
2 sprigs parsley

1. Wipe meat with damp cloth; place in large deep kettle; cover with cold water.

2. Add remaining ingredients.

3. Cover; bring to a boil; reduce heat to low; simmer 3½–5 hours or until meat is tender; remove any scum which appears.

4. Remove from stock; slice; serve with horseradish sauce.

NEW ENGLAND BOILED DINNER

1. About 45 minutes before corned beef is done, add 6 pared potatoes, carrots, white turnips, cover; boil 15 minutes.

2. Add 1 medium head cabbage, cut into quarters; cover; cook only until vegetables are just tender.

VEAL RECIPES

Temperature-Time Chart For Roast Veal

325° F. Oven Temperature

Use rack in uncovered roaster.
Add no water.
Do not baste.

Cut	Approximate Minutes Per Pound 3-6 Pounds	Approximate Minutes Per Pound 6-8 Pounds	Meat Thermometer Reading When Roast Is Done
Leg, Round, Rump	35–40	30	180° F.
Loin	35	30	180° F.
Shoulder			
Bone In	40	35	180° F.
Boned	45	40	180° F.

ROAST VEAL

1. Wipe meat with damp cloth to remove any loose small pieces of bone.

2. Rub meat, if desired, with cut side of clove of garlic.

3. Place fat side up on rack in open roasting pan.

4. Lay several strips bacon or salt pork over roast to provide additional fat and flavor.

5. If using a meat thermometer, insert it into center of thickest part of roast being certain bulb does not rest on bone, fat or gristle.

6. Sprinkle with salt, pepper.

7. Do not flour; add no water; do not baste during roasting period.

8. Roast according to chart.

VEAL Recipes

ROAST STUFFED LOIN OF VEAL

- 3½ pounds loin of veal, with pocket
- 2 cups fine bread crumbs
- 1 small onion, minced
- ½ cup diced celery
- 2 tablespoons butter
- ¼ cup hot water
- ¼ cup grated American cheese
- 1 teaspoon salt
- ¼ teaspoon pepper
- 4 strips bacon

1. Wipe meat with damp cloth.
2. To make stuffing, combine crumbs, onion, celery; moisten with butter melted in water; add cheese, salt, pepper.
3. Place stuffing in pocket; sew or fasten with skewers.
4. Place on rack in open roasting pan; add no water; do not cover.
5. Place bacon strips over veal.
6. Roast 2 hours in moderate oven 325° F.
7. Eight servings.

BRAISED VEAL CHOPS

- ¼ cup flour
- ½ teaspoon salt
- ⅛ teaspoon pepper
- 4 loin or rib veal chops, ¾ inch thick
- 2 tablespoons fat
- 1¼ cups water, tomato juice or sauterne wine
- 2 tablespoons flour
- 3 tablespoons cold water
- Salt
- Pepper

1. Combine flour, salt, pepper; coat chops.
2. Melt fat in heavy fry pan.
3. Add chops; sauté until well browned on both sides.
4. Add liquid; cover; simmer 45–50 minutes or until meat is tender.
5. Remove chops to hot platter; remove pan from heat.
6. Combine flour, cold water to make paste; add ¼ cup liquid from pan to paste.
7. Stir paste into remaining liquid; return to heat; cook, stirring constantly until gravy bubbles.
8. Add seasoning to taste; pour over chops.
9. Four servings.

Variations

1. Use half sour cream, half water for liquid.
2. Add sautéed mushrooms to the gravy.
3. Sprinkle chopped parsley or chives over chops.

VEAL Recipes

VEAL POT ROAST

1. Heat heavy fry pan or Dutch Oven over medium high heat until a piece of white paper placed in bottom turns brown.
2. Add piece of veal shoulder boned, rolled, tied; brown on all sides.
3. Sprinkle with salt, pepper.
4. Cover; cook over low heat, allowing about 30–35 minutes per pound.
5. If desired, ½ cup hot water may be added after meat is browned although this is not necessary as meat will cook in its own juices.

VEAL FRICASSEE

2 pounds cubed veal, rump
¼ cup flour
2 tablespoons fat
½ cup hot water
½ cup diced onion
½ cup diced celery
1 cup cubed raw potatoes
1 cup sliced raw carrots
1½ teaspoons salt
¼ teaspoon pepper

1. Roll veal in flour; brown in Dutch Oven or heavy fry pan; add remaining ingredients.
2. Cover; cook over low heat 30–35 minutes.
3. If necessary, add more water during cooking; thicken gravy if desired.
4. Four servings.

SPANISH VEAL CHOPS

3 tablespoons flour
1 teaspoon salt
¼ teaspoon pepper
6 loin or rib veal chops
5 tablespoons fat, drippings
1 cup sliced, peeled onions
1 cup canned tomatoes
½ cup water
1 tablespoon chopped parsley
1 bay leaf
1 teaspoon salt
½ teaspoon pepper
2 tablespoons cornstarch
½ cup cold water

1. Combine flour, salt, pepper; coat chops.
2. Melt fat in heavy fry pan; add chops; brown thoroughly on both sides; remove to warm platter.
3. Sauté onions in fat 5 minutes; place chops on top of onions.
4. Add tomatoes, water, parsley, bay leaf, salt, pepper.
5. Cover; simmer one hour.
6. Remove chops to platter.
7. Mix cornstarch, water to smooth paste; add a little liquid from pan; add paste to remaining liquid; cook until thickened; pour over chops.
8. Four servings.

VEAL Recipes

BREADED VEAL CUTLET

- **2 pounds veal cutlet, ½ inch thick**
- **1 cup dry crumbs**
- **½ teaspoon salt**
- **⅛ teaspoon pepper**
- **1 egg, beaten**
- **¼ cup milk**
- **4 tablespoons butter or margarine**

1. Cut veal into serving pieces.

2. Combine crumbs, salt, pepper.

3. Combine egg, milk.

4. Dip veal into crumbs, then into egg mixture and into crumbs again.

5. Place breaded veal in refrigerator 30 minutes.

6. When ready to use, melt fat in heavy fry pan.

7. Add meat; cook slowly about 15 minutes on each side until browned.

8. Four servings.

Variations

1. Pour can of tomato sauce over meat after browning; cover; simmer 15 minutes.

2. Pour can of mushroom, celery or chicken soup over meat after browning; cover; simmer 15 minutes.

3. Pour one pint sour cream over meat after browning; cover; simmer 5 minutes.

4. Brush veal with French dressing before dipping into crumb-egg mixture.

5. Rub veal with cut side of clove of garlic before breading.

VEAL AU GRATIN WITH OLIVES

- **3 tablespoons shortening**
- **4 tablespoons flour**
- **2 cups milk**
- **½ teaspoon salt**
- **⅛ teaspoon pepper**
- **½ teaspoon nutmeg**
- **¼ teaspoon ginger**
- **2 cups cooked diced veal**
- **1 cup quartered stuffed olives**
- **½ cup canned mushrooms**
- **2 tablespoons dry bread crumbs**
- **4 tablespoons grated American or Parmesan cheese**

1. Melt shortening in sauce pan; remove from heat; add flour; blend.

2. Add milk; cook over low heat, stirring constantly until thickened.

3. Add salt, pepper, nutmeg, ginger; stir until blended.

4. Combine veal, olives, mushrooms; place in greased casserole or 8″ x 8″ x 2″ cake pan.

5. Pour creamed mixture over meat.

6. Sprinkle with crumbs, cheese.

7. Bake 35–40 minutes in moderate oven 375° F.

8. Six servings.

VEAL Recipes

VEAL CHOP SUEY

1 pound cubed veal
¼ cup flour
2 tablespoons fat
2 tablespoons hot water
1 cup diced celery
½ cup diced green pepper
½ cup diced onion
1 teaspoon salt
⅛ teaspoon pepper
1½ teaspoons soy sauce
1 bouillon cube
1½ cups hot water

1. Roll veal in flour; brown in hot fat in Dutch Oven; add water.
2. Cover; simmer 5 minutes.
3. Add remaining ingredients; cover; cook over low heat 35–40 minutes.
4. Thicken juices if desired; serve over rice.
5. Six servings.

VEAL STEW WITH DUMPLINGS

1. Follow recipe for Beef Stew (page 41), substituting cubed veal shoulder for beef.
2. Sift 1 cup all purpose flour, 2 teaspoons baking powder, 1 teaspoon salt together; beat 1 egg; add ½ cup milk, 2 tablespoons melted butter; add to flour; beat until smooth. Drop from tablespoon on top of stew.
3. Cover; cook 15 minutes; do not lift cover during time dumplings are cooking.
4. If spoon is dipped into hot stew, then into batter, dumplings will slide off easily.

STUFFED VEAL CUTLET

2 large veal cutlets, ¾ inch thick
Salt
Pepper
6 cups stale bread cubes
¾ teaspoon salt
⅛ teaspoon pepper
1½ teaspoons sage or poultry seasoning
1 tablespoon minced parsley
1 tablespoon minced celery
5 tablespoons butter, melted
¼ cup minced onion
1½ cups cream of mushroom soup

1. Spread cutlets flat; sprinkle with salt, pepper.
2. Combine bread, seasonings, parsley, celery.
3. Melt butter in Dutch Oven; add onion; sauté 5 minutes.
4. Add bread mixture; cook 2 minutes over low heat, stirring constantly.
5. Divide stuffing into 2 portions; place one portion on one half of each cutlet; fold other half over; fasten edges together with toothpicks or poultry pins; lace with cord.
6. Place cutlets in Dutch Oven; brown on both sides, adding fat if necessary.
7. Pour mushroom soup over meat.
8. Cover; cook over low heat 45–50 minutes or until meat is tender.
9. Four servings.

VEAL Recipes

VEAL SAUTÉ WITH MUSHROOMS IN RICE RING

2 pounds cubed veal
½ cup flour
4 tablespoons butter
1¼ cups boiling water
1 tablespoon Worcestershire Sauce
1 cup diced canned mushrooms
1 teaspoon salt
⅛ teaspoon pepper

1. Coat veal with flour.
2. Melt butter in heavy fry pan; add meat; brown on all sides.
3. Add water, Worcestershire Sauce, mushrooms, salt, pepper; mix.
4. Cover; cook over low heat 35–40 minutes.
5. Fill buttered ring mold with cooked rice, patting it firmly.
6. Turn mold onto platter; put meat mixture into center.
7. Garnish rice with minced parsley.
8. Six servings.

VEAL SHORTCAKE

2 cups cubed cooked leftover veal
3 tablespoons flour
2 tablespoons minced onion
1 cup diced celery
¼ cup butter
2 cups milk
1 teaspoon salt
1 teaspoon Worcestershire Sauce
Hot baking powder biscuits

1. Roll veal in flour; brown lightly with onion, celery in butter.
2. Add milk slowly; cook over low heat until thickened, stirring constantly.
3. Add salt, Worcestershire Sauce.
4. Split hot biscuits; butter; place on platter with meat mixture between the halves.
5. Four servings.

VEAL BIRDS

1½ pounds veal cutlet ½ inch thick
1 cup bread stuffing
6 slices bacon
2 tablespoons fat
1 cup hot water
2 tablespoons flour
¼ cup cold water

1. Cut cutlets into 6 pieces 2″ x 4″.
2. Place about 2 tablespoons bread stuffing in center of each.
3. Roll; wrap slice of bacon around each bird; fasten with toothpicks.
4. Melt fat in heavy fry pan; add birds; brown on all sides.
5. Add water; cover; cook over low heat 50–60 minutes.
6. Make paste of flour, water; combine with liquid in pan to make gravy.
7. Six servings.

VEAL Recipes

VEAL SCALLOPINI

6 thin slices veal shank
6 tablespoons flour
4 tablespoons butter
3 medium onions, sliced thin
1 clove garlic, minced
2 bouillon cubes
1 cup boiling water
1 teaspoon dry mustard
3 teaspoons paprika
3 tablespoons minced parsley
4 tablespoons butter
1 cup sour cream

1. Dust veal with flour.
2. Melt butter in heavy fry pan; add onions, garlic; cook until yellow.
3. Add bouillon cubes, water; stir until cubes dissolve; add mustard, paprika; stir, pour into bowl; set aside.
4. Melt 4 additional tablespoons butter in fry pan; add floured meat; cook until browned on both sides.
5. Pour onion mixture over meat; cover; cook over low heat 30 minutes.
6. Stir in cream; bring to boil; remove from heat.
7. Four servings.

VEAL PAPRIKA

4 pounds veal shoulder boned, rolled, tied
1½ tablespoons butter
1 tablespoon paprika
¼ cup flour
1 teaspoon salt
2 tablespoons shortening
1 medium onion, minced
¾ cup finely diced celery
¼ cup water
2 tablespoons flour
½ cup sweet or sour cream

1. Wipe meat with damp cloth; brown on all sides in heavy fry pan or Dutch Oven.
2. Cream butter; add paprika, flour, salt to make a paste; spread over browned meat.
3. Cover; cook over low heat one hour.
4. Melt shortening in another fry pan; add onion; cook until lightly browned; add celery, water; cover; cook 8–10 minutes.
5. After veal has cooked one hour, pour onion-celery mixture over top; cook one hour longer or until meat is tender.
6. Stir flour into cream; combine with juice in pan; spoon over veal; cover; cook 15 minutes longer.
7. Eight servings.

LAMB RECIPES

Temperature-Time Chart For Roast Lamb

325° F. Oven Temperature

Use rack in uncovered roaster.
Add no water.
Do not baste.

Cut	Weight Pounds	Approximate Minutes Per Pound	Meat Thermometer Reading When Roast Is Done
Leg			
Unboned	4–6	35–40	182° F.
	6–7	30–35	182° F.
Boned, Rolled	3–5	45	182° F.
	5–6	40–45	182° F.
Loin	2½–3	50	182° F.
Cushion			
Shoulder, Stuffed	3–4	40–45	
Rolled Shoulder	3½–5	40–45	182° F.
Sirloin Half of Leg	2–3	60	
Crown of Lamb (no stuffing)	3–4	40–45	182° F.

ROAST LAMB

1. Wipe meat with damp cloth; do not remove the "fell", a thin papery skin, from a leg of lamb.

2. Rub with cut side of a clove of garlic.

3. Sprinkle with salt, pepper.

4. Place, fat side up, on rack in open roasting pan.

5. If using a meat thermometer, insert it into thickest part, being sure bulb does not rest on bone, fat or gristle.

6. Do not flour; add no water; do not baste during roasting.

7. Roast according to temperature-time chart.

LAMB Recipes

CROWN ROAST OF LAMB

1. Have butcher shape two or more rib sections into a "crown."

2. Remove any ground trimmings butcher may have placed in center; use these for patties or meat loaf.

3. Cover ends of bones with cubes of bread or salt pork; remove these before serving.

4. Sprinkle with salt, pepper.

5. Place on rack in open roasting pan.

6. Roast according to temperature-time chart.

7. To serve: fill center with mashed potatoes, buttered peas, buttered peas and carrots, buttered cauliflower or buttered peas and mushrooms.

8. Allow 2–3 ribs per person.

LAMB POT ROAST

4 pounds lamb shoulder boned, rolled, tied
Clove of garlic
Salt, pepper

1. Rub meat with cut side of clove of garlic.

2. Heat Dutch Oven over medium high heat until piece of white paper placed in bottom turns golden brown.

3. Add meat; brown thoroughly on all sides.

4. Sprinkle with salt, pepper.

5. Cover; cook over low heat 2–2½ hours or until meat is tender.

6. Potatoes, carrots may be added during last hour of cooking.

7. Eight servings.

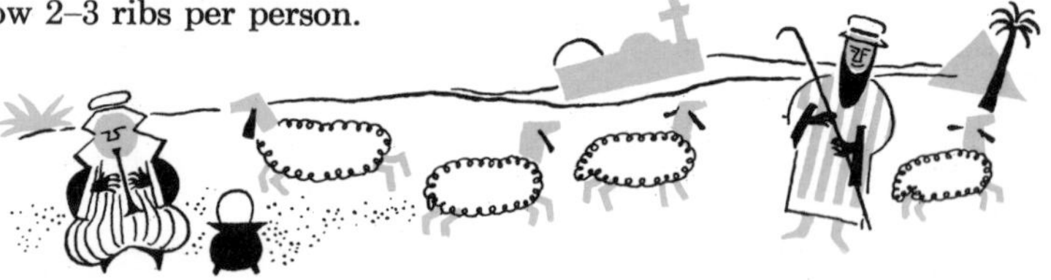

Broiling Time Table For Lamb Chops and Patties

Turn after broiling ½ the time

Cut	Thickness	Approximate Broiling Time
Patties from Ground Lamb	¾ inch	14–15 minutes
Rib or Loin Chops	¾–1 inch	14–16 minutes
Double Chops	1½ inches 2 inches	20–25 minutes 36–40 minutes
English Chops	1½ inches 2 inches	20–25 minutes 36–40 minutes
Shoulder Chops	¾–1 inch 1½ inches	14–16 minutes 20–25 minutes

LAMB Recipes

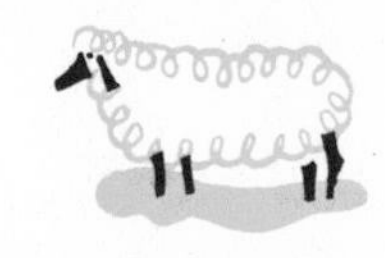

PANBROILED CHOPS and PATTIES

1. Heat heavy aluminum fry pan over medium high heat until a piece of white paper placed in bottom turns brown.

2. Add meat; allow to brown on one side; turn; brown second side; continue to turn; cook to degree of doneness desired.

3. Sprinkle with salt, pepper.

MAGGIE'S LAMB CHOPS

4 loin lamb chops, 1 inch thick
Salt, pepper
4 slices American cheese
4 slices Bermuda onion
8 tablespoons thick sour cream

1. Wrap tail end of each chop around thick part to form a flat round patty; fasten with toothpicks.

2. Sprinkle with salt, pepper.

3. Place chops in shallow baking pan.

4. Place one slice cheese, one slice onion on each chop.

5. Put 2 tablespoons sour cream on each chop.

6. Add no water; do not cover.

7. Bake 1 hour in moderate oven 375° F.

8. Four servings.

DORIS' LAMB CHOPS

2 hard cooked eggs, shelled
½ cup butter
6 tablespoons fine dry bread crumbs
2 teaspoons minced onion
1 teaspoon salt
¼ teaspoon pepper
1 teaspoon Worcestershire Sauce
4 loin lamb chops, 1 inch thick

1. Chop whites of eggs fine; rub yolks through sieve.

2. Melt butter in fry pan; add crumbs, onion; cook until lightly browned.

3. Add salt, pepper, Worcestershire Sauce, eggs; blend well.

4. Sprinkle chops with salt, pepper.

5. Pat crumb mixture on one side of each chop; place a square of Alcoa Wrap, waxed or parchment paper on top; turn; pat mixture on second side.

6. Wrap foil or paper around each chop.

7. Place in shallow baking pan; add no water; do not cover.

8. Bake 1 hour in moderate oven 375° F.

9. To serve: unwrap chops; place on platter; garnish with spiced peaches, parsley.

10. Four servings.

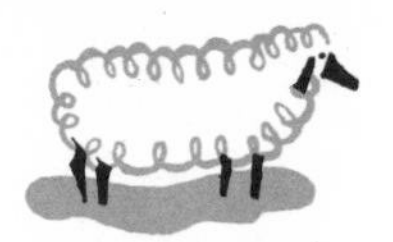

LAMB Recipes

LAMB and RED BEAN GOULASH

2 teaspoons salt
½ teaspoon pepper
4 tablespoons flour
2 pounds lamb shank, cubed
2 tablespoons fat
1 clove garlic, minced
¼ cup diced onion
2½ cups canned tomatoes
1 green pepper, diced
1 teaspoon salt
2 cans red kidney beans

1. Combine salt, pepper, flour; add meat; toss until coated.
2. Melt fat in Dutch Oven; add meat; brown on all sides.
3. Add garlic, onion, tomatoes, green pepper, salt.
4. Cover; simmer 1½ hours.
5. Drain kidney beans; add; cook 5 minutes longer.
6. Four servings.

JULIENNE LAMB and MUSHROOMS

2 pounds boneless lamb shoulder
6 tablespoons flour
3 tablespoons fat
1½ teaspoons salt
¼ teaspoon ground cloves
½ cup water
½ pound sliced fresh mushrooms
1 cup milk
1 No. 2 can Chinese noodles

1. Cut lamb into 3 inch strips; roll in flour; brown in fat.
2. Add salt, cloves, water.
3. Cover; cook over low heat 1 hour.
4. Add mushrooms; cook 15 minutes longer.
5. Add milk; cook until juices in pan are slightly thickened.
6. Serve over Chinese noodles.
7. Eight servings.

LAMB CURRY

1¼ cups washed uncooked rice
1 cup sliced, peeled onions
2¼ cups diced celery
4 tablespoons fat
1 tablespoon flour
4½ cups cubed, cooked lamb
1½–2 teaspoons curry powder
1¼ cups lamb gravy
½ cup hot water
Salt

1. Cook rice in boiling salted water until tender; rinse; drain.
2. Sauté onions, celery in fat in heavy fry pan until tender.
3. Stir in flour; add lamb, curry powder, gravy, water, salt.
4. Cover; cook over low heat 10–15 minutes.
5. Serve over the rice or use rice as border around meat mixture.
6. Six servings.

LAMB Recipes

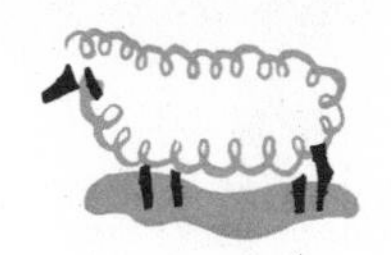

IRISH STEW

- **3 pounds lamb cut into small pieces**
- **Water to cover**
- **4 allspice berries**
- **2 tablespoons minced parsley**
- **1 cup sliced carrots**
- **¾ cup diced turnips**
- **3 cups cubed potatoes**
- **½ cup sliced onion**
- **Salt**
- **Pepper**

1. Place meat in Dutch Oven; add water to cover; add allspice berries, parsley; cover; simmer 2 hours.

2. Add vegetables, salt, pepper.

3. Cover; cook 35–45 minutes longer.

4. Thicken gravy if desired. Drop dumplings may be added 15 minutes before cooking is completed.

5. Eight servings.

LAMB SUPREME

- **2 pounds boneless lamb shoulder**
- **2 tablespoons fat**
- **Water to cover**
- **½ teaspoon salt**
- **½ teaspoon dill seeds**
- **½ cup sliced fresh mushrooms**
- **1 cup sour cream**
- **½ teaspoon vinegar**
- **3 tablespoons flour**

1. Cut lamb into cubes; brown in hot fat in heavy fry pan.

2. Add water to cover, salt, dill seeds; cover.

3. Simmer over low heat 1½ hours or until meat is tender.

4. Remove meat; add mushrooms, cream, vinegar to liquid in pan; cook 15 minutes.

5. Add flour to liquid; stir; add meat; heat through.

6. Six servings.

LAMB RIBLETS with VEGETABLES

- **2 tablespoons fat**
- **3 pounds breast of lamb, cut into riblets**
- **2 teaspoons salt**
- **⅛ teaspoon pepper**
- **1½ cups water**
- **6–8 small white onions**
- **8 whole carrots**
- **1 pound green beans**
- **¼ cup vinegar**

1. Melt fat in Dutch Oven; add lamb; brown on all sides.

2. Add salt, pepper, water, cover; simmer 45 minutes.

3. Add vegetables; cook 30 minutes.

4. Add vinegar; cook 30 minutes longer.

5. To serve: pile meat in center of platter; arrange vegetables around edge.

6. Six servings.

PORK RECIPES

Temperature-Time Chart For Roast Fresh Pork
325° F. Oven Temperature

Use rack in uncovered roaster.
Add no water
Do not baste.

Cut	Weight Pounds	Approximate Minutes Per Pound	Meat Thermometer Reading When Roast Is Done
Boston Butt	3–6	50–55	185° F.
Fresh Ham	3–6	45–50	185° F.
	6–8	40–45	185° F.
Loin	3–6	35–40	185° F.
	6–8	35–38	
Picnic Shoulder	3–6	40	185° F.
	6–8	35	185° F.
Crown of Pork (no filling)	6–7	40–45	185° F.

ROAST FRESH PORK

1. Wipe meat with damp cloth.
2. Rub with cut side of clove of garlic.
3. Sprinkle with salt, pepper.
4. Place, fat side up, on rack in open roasting pan.
5. If using a meat thermometer, insert it into thickest part, being sure bulb does not rest on bone, fat or gristle.
6. Do not flour; add no water; do not baste during roasting.
7. Roast according to temperature-time chart for fresh pork.

PORK Recipes

CROWN ROAST OF PORK

1. Have butcher shape two or more sections into "crown."
2. Cover ends of bones with cubes of bread or salt pork; remove these before serving.
3. Place on rack in open roasting pan.
4. Fill center with bread stuffing if desired.
5. Roast according to temperature-time chart.
6. To serve; if bread stuffing is not used, fill center with mashed potatoes, mashed sweet potatoes or buttered vegetables.
7. Allow 2–3 ribs per person.

SPANISH PORK CHOPS

4 loin pork chops, 1 inch thick
Salt, pepper
4 slices onion
4 tablespoons ketchup
½ cup diluted vinegar or sweet pickle juice

1. Place chops in shallow baking pan.
2. Sprinkle with salt, pepper.
3. Place slice of onion on each chop; top with ketchup.
4. Pour vinegar or pickle juice around chops.
5. Bake 1 hour or until tender in moderate oven 350° F.
6. Four servings.

BAKED STUFFED PORK CHOPS

1 cup diced apples
¼ cup seedless raisins
¾ cup soft bread crumbs
¾ teaspoon salt
1½ tablespoons sugar
1 tablespoon minced onion
2 tablespoons butter
3 tablespoons hot water
4 rib chops, 1½ inches thick with pocket
Salt, pepper
½ cup water

1. Mix together apples, raisins, bread crumbs, salt, sugar.
2. Sauté onion in butter 5 minutes; add to bread mixture.
3. Add hot water; blend.
4. Sprinkle salt, pepper on inside of pocket.
5. Fill pockets with stuffing; fasten with toothpicks or poultry pins.
6. Brown chops well on both sides.
7. Place in casserole or 8″ x 8″ x 2″ cake pan.
8. Add water to drippings in fry pan; stir to loosen brown sediment; pour around chops.
9. Cover casserole or use Alcoa Wrap on cake pan.
10. Bake 1 hour in moderate oven 375° F.; uncover last 15 minutes.
11. Four servings.

PORK Recipes

SWEET-SOUR PORK

1½ pounds leftover pork, sliced
½ cup water
⅓ cup vinegar
¼ cup brown sugar
2 tablespoons cornstarch
½ teaspoon salt
1 No. 2 can pineapple chunks
1 medium green pepper, thinly sliced
2 medium onions, thinly sliced

1. Brown meat lightly in melted fat.
2. Combine water, vinegar, sugar, cornstarch, salt, 1 cup pineapple juice drained from chunks.
3. Cook in sauce pan until clear and slightly thickened.
4. Pour sauce over meat; cover; cook 30 minutes.
5. Add pineapple chunks, green pepper, onion; cook 2 minutes longer.
6. Serve with fried rice.
7. Four servings.

BREADED PORK CHOPS

4 loin pork chops
Seasoned fine dry crumbs or corn meal
1 egg, beaten
2 tablespoons milk
4 tablespoons fat
½ cup water

1. Roll chops in crumbs; dip into beaten egg combined with milk, then into crumbs.
2. Melt fat in heavy fry pan; add chops; brown slowly on both sides.
3. Add water; cover; cook over low heat 35–45 minutes or until meat is tender.
4. More water may be added if necessary.

BRIDE'S DINNER

5 slices day-old bread, cubed
1 egg yolk, beaten
1 tablespoon melted butter
½ teaspoon salt
⅛ teaspoon pepper
⅛ teaspoon poultry seasoning
1 teaspoon grated onion
4 pork chops, 1 inch thick
4 medium baking apples
¼ cup seedless raisins
4 tablespoons sugar
¼ teaspoon cinnamon
4 medium sweet potatoes, pared
3 tablespoons melted butter
Salt, pepper

1. Combine bread cubes, egg yolk, butter, seasonings, onion; shape into 4 balls.
2. Place chops in shallow baking pan; sprinkle with salt, pepper.
3. Place one ball of stuffing on each chop.
4. Core apples; set in pan with chops.
5. Combine raisins, sugar, cinnamon; fill centers of apples.
6. Roll sweet potatoes in melted butter; place in pan with chops, apples; sprinkle with salt, pepper.
7. Bake 1½ hours in moderate oven 350° F.
8. Four servings.

PORK Recipes

BAKED PORK CHOPS

4 pork chops, ½ inch thick
2 tablespoons fat
¼ cup diced onion
1 cup condensed cream of celery soup
½ cup milk
3 medium potatoes, peeled, sliced
1 pound cabbage, shredded
¼ cup flour
1½ teaspoons salt
⅛ tespoon pepper

1. Brown chops in hot fat in heavy fry pan; remove.

2. Add onion, soup, milk to fat in pan; blend; set aside.

3. Starting with potatoes, put alternate layers of potatoes, cabbage, into a 2-quart casserole or 8″ x 8″ x 2″ cake pan; sprinkle each layer with flour; pour soup sauce over each layer.

4. Place chops on top; cover casserole or use Alcoa Wrap to cover pan.

5. Bake 1¼ hours in moderate oven 350° F.

6. Four servings.

PORK CHOPS with ORANGE SAUCE

6 loin pork chops, ¾ inch thick
1 tablespoon butter
1 medium onion, diced
1 tablespoon flour
2 bouillon cubes
1 cup hot water
½ teaspoon minced parsley
1 drop oil of peppermint
1 teaspoon dry mustard
2 tablespoons lemon juice
½ cup orange juice
1 teaspoon salt
⅛ teaspoon pepper

1. Heat aluminum fry pan over medium high heat until a piece of white paper placed in bottom turns golden brown.

2. Add chops; brown on both sides; remove from pan.

3. Melt butter; add onion; sauté 5 minutes.

4. Stir in flour; dissolve bouillon cubes in hot water; add slowly, stirring constantly; cook 5 minutes.

5. Add parsley, peppermint oil, lemon and orange juice, salt, pepper; blend thoroughly.

6. Place chops in liquid; cover; cook over low heat 25–35 minutes or until meat is tender.

7. Six servings.

PORK Recipes

PORK CHOPS ALEXANDER

1 cup dried apricots
2 cups warm water
½ cup flour
½ teaspoon salt
¼ teaspoon pepper
¼ teaspoon thyme
6 loin pork chops, ¾ inch thick
3 tablespoons fat
¼ cup maple syrup

1. Cook apricots in water until tender; drain.
2. Combine flour, salt, pepper, thyme; dust over both sides of chops.
3. Brown chops on both sides in hot fat in heavy fry pan.
4. Combine apricots, maple syrup; pour over chops.
5. Cover; cook 1 hour over low heat until chops are tender.
6. Six servings.

BRAISED PORK CHOPS

1. Heat aluminum fry pan over medium high heat until a piece of white paper placed in bottom turns brown.
2. Add chops; brown slowly on both sides.
3. Cover; cook over low heat 35–40 minutes until tender.
4. Pork should always be cooked until well done. For this reason, pork chops should never be broiled or just panbroiled.

SAUCY SAUSAGES

1½ pounds bulk fresh pork sausage
2 medium onions, sliced
1 tablespoon flour
½ cup milk
½ cup water
2 tablespoons vinegar
1 bay leaf
¼ teaspoon dry mustard
⅛ teaspoon cloves
¼ teaspoon pepper
½ teaspoon salt

1. Shape meat into 6 patties; brown in heavy fry pan; remove; drain on absorbent paper.
2. Brown onion slightly in sausage drippings; remove.
3. Drain off all but 2 tablespoons of drippings.
4. Stir in flour until smooth; gradually add milk, water, vinegar; add bay leaf, mustard, cloves, pepper, salt; cook, stirring constantly until thickened.
5. Return meat, onions to sauce; simmer over low heat 5 minutes.
6. Serve over steamed rice.
7. Six servings.

PORK Recipes

FRESH PORK SAUSAGE

1 pound link sausage or patties
½ cup water

1. Place links or patties in *cold* fry pan; add water; cover; bring to boil; simmer 5–10 minutes depending upon thickness.
2. Drain; cook uncovered over medium heat until golden brown and all pink has disappeared.
3. Keep draining off fat as sausage cooks.
4. Turn frequently using cake turner as fork will pierce skin.
5. Four servings.

SAUSAGE LOAVES

1 pound bulk fresh pork sausage
¾ cup milk
1½ cups dry bread crumbs
1 teaspoon finely minced onion
2 tablespoons ketchup
2 tablespoons horseradish
2 teaspoons prepared mustard
1 egg, beaten

1. Combine ingredients; mix well.
2. Pack into 12 muffin cups.
3. Bake 1½ hours in moderate oven 350° F.
4. Six servings.

AMERICAN PIZZA

1 pound bulk fresh sausage
⅛ teaspoon thyme
½ clove garlic
2 cups biscuit mix
½ cup milk
1 cup grated American cheese
1½ cups drained canned tomatoes

1. Brown sausage in fry pan; drain off fat; add thyme, garlic.
2. Combine biscuit mix, milk to make soft dough.
3. Roll on floured board to fit 9 inch pie pan.
4. Fit dough into pan; crimp edges.
5. Pour meat into pan; add cheese; top with tomatoes.
6. Bake 25 minutes in hot oven 450° F.
7. If desired, sprinkle with Parmesan cheese before baking.
8. Six servings.

CRUSTY SAUSAGE CAKES

1 pound bulk fresh pork sausage
1 egg, beaten
2 tablespoons water
2 cups crushed corn flakes

1. Shape sausage into four patties.
2. Dip into egg combined with water.
3. Roll in corn flakes.
4. Place in fry pan; cook slowly, turning frequently over low heat until browned and thoroughly done.
5. Four servings.

PORK Recipes

SAUSAGE UPSIDE DOWN PIE

- 1 pound bulk fresh pork sausage
- 2 tablespoons water
- 2 medium onions, sliced
- ¾ cup condensed tomato soup
- ¾ cup water
- ⅔ cup milk
- 2 cups prepared biscuit mix

1. Shape meat into 6 patties.
2. Place in fry pan; add water; cover; simmer 15 minutes.
3. Remove cover; brown patties on both sides.
4. Place patties in casserole or 8″ x 8″ x 2″ cake pan.
5. Brown onion rings in sausage drippings.
6. Place onions on patties; pour on tomato soup combined with water.
7. Combine milk, biscuit mix; blend to make soft dough.
8. Roll to fit baking dish; place on top of meat mixture; brush lightly with milk.
9. Bake 20 minutes in moderate oven 400° F.
10. Six servings.

HUNGARIAN SAUSAGE LOAF

- 1 cup diced mushrooms
- 2 tablespoons butter
- 1 egg, beaten
- 1 pound bulk fresh pork sausage
- 2 cups dry bread crumbs
- 1 teaspoon paprika

1. Sauté mushrooms in butter in fry pan.
2. Combine mushrooms, egg, bread crumbs; shape into loaf; sprinkle with paprika.
3. Place in small roaster; bake covered ½ hour in moderate oven 350° F.; remove cover; bake 30 minutes longer.
4. Four servings.

SPARERIBS AND SAUERKRAUT

- 3 pounds spareribs
- 2 tablespoons fat
- 2 large onions, sliced
- ¼ teaspoon salt
- ⅛ teaspoon pepper
- ½ cup hot water
- 2 pounds sauerkraut

1. Brown ribs in hot fat in Dutch Oven.
2. Add onion, salt, pepper, water.
3. Cover; simmer over low heat 1 hour.
4. Add sauerkraut; cover; cook 20 minutes longer.
5. Four servings.

PORK Recipes

HAWAIIAN RIBS

- 4 pounds spareribs, cut into 1½ inch strips
- ¾ cup cornstarch
- ¼ cup molasses
- ¼ cup soy sauce
- ½ cup sugar
- ¾ cup vinegar
- ¾ cup water
- ¾ cup pineapple juice
- 1 can pineapple chunks
- 2 green peppers, cut into 1 inch cubes

1. Brown ribs in heavy fry pan or Dutch Oven.
2. Combine cornstarch, molasses, soy sauce to make paste.
3. Spread paste on both sides of each piece of ribs.
4. Rebrown quickly in hot fat.
5. Combine sugar, vinegar, water, pineapple juice; heat until sugar dissolves; pour over ribs.
6. Cover; cook 25–30 minutes.
7. Add pineapple chunks, green pepper cubes; recover; simmer 5 minutes longer.
8. Eight servings.

BARBECUED SPARERIBS

- 4 pounds spareribs
- 1 clove garlic
- 1 large onion, diced
- 2 tablespoons butter
- 1 cup canned tomatoes
- 1 cup diced celery
- 1 cup diced green pepper
- 1 cup ketchup
- 2 tablespoons brown sugar
- 3 dashes Tabasco Sauce
- ½ teaspoon dry mustard
- 2 cups beef stock or 2 bouillon cubes dissolved in 2 cups boiling water
- Salt, pepper

1. Rub ribs with cut side of clove of garlic.
2. Place in shallow baking pan; roast uncovered 30 minutes in moderate oven 350° F.
3. Brown onion in melted butter in heavy fry pan.
4. Add remaining ingredients; stir; cover.
5. Simmer over low heat 1 hour.
6. After ribs have roasted the 30 minutes, pour sauce over top.
7. Roast 45 minutes longer, basting frequently.
8. Four servings.

PORK Recipes

STUFFED SPARERIBS

2 pounds spareribs
Salt, pepper
1½ cups soft bread crumbs
1 medium onion, minced
2 tablespoons minced parsley
1 tablespoon melted butter
1 tablespoon water
½ teaspoon salt
⅛ teaspoon pepper
2 tablespoons fat
1 cup hot water

1. Rub ribs with salt, pepper.
2. Combine bread crumbs, onion, parsley, butter, water, salt, pepper; mix.
3. Spread over half of ribs; place other half on top; fasten together with skewers or sew together with cord.
4. Brown on both sides in hot fat in Dutch Oven.
5. Add hot water; cover; simmer 1½–2 hours over low heat.
6. Four servings.

OVEN BROILED BACON

1. Preheat broiler with pan 3–3½ inches below heat.
2. Place bacon strips on rack of broiler pan.
3. Broil 2–2½ minutes to a side or until done, turning only once.

PANBROILED BACON

1. Place bacon strips in cold fry pan; place over medium low heat; cook slowly, turning once.
2. Drain off fat as it accumulates if you want bacon to be crisp.

ROAST CANADIAN BACON

1½ pounds Canadian bacon
Whole cloves
⅓ cup brown sugar
1½ tablespoons prepared mustard
1 cup canned pineapple juice

1. Remove casing from Canadian bacon.
2. Score fat side with sharp knife; stud with cloves.
3. Combine sugar, mustard to make paste; spread over meat.
4. Place in shallow baking pan; pour pineapple juice around sides.
5. Bake 1 hour or 35 minutes per pound in moderate oven 350° F.
6. Six servings.

HAM RECIPES

Temperature-Time Chart For Baking Uncooked Mild Cure Smoked Hams

325° F. Oven Temperature

Weight of Ham	Approximate Minutes Per Pound	Meat Thermometer Reading When Ham Is Done
Bone In		
5– 8 pounds half ham (butt or shank)	26–28	160° F.
8–10 pounds whole ham	25–26	160° F.
10–12 pounds whole ham	23–24	160° F.
12–15 pounds whole ham	21–22	160° F.
15–18 pounds whole ham	20	160° F.
Picnic Shoulder	30–35	170° F.
Bone Out		
Half Ham	28	160° F.
Whole Ham	23	160° F.
Boneless Shank End	32–34	160° F.

HAM

Most national brand hams today are of the mild cure smoked type. They are either uncooked or are cooked, ready to eat.

HAM Recipes

UNCOOKED MILD CURE SMOKED HAMS

1. Require no soaking or parboiling.

2. Cook in much less time.

3. Must be kept in refrigerator before and after cooking.

4. Available, *whole with bone in.* These are known as "regular" and have the skin left on. The wrapper is usually marked "Cook Before Eating."

5. Available, *whole with bone out.* These have been boned, rolled and tied or put into a transparent casing which is removed after baking.

COOKED SMOKED HAMS

1. Require no soaking or parboiling.

2. Need only to be heated for serving or may be served "as is."

3. Available, *whole with bone in.* These are labeled "Ready to Eat, Cooked or Fully Cooked."

4. Available, *whole with bone out.* These have been boned, rolled, tied or pressed and are labeled "Ready to Eat."

TO BAKE WHOLE OR HALF UNCOOKED MILD CURE SMOKED HAMS

If packer's wrapper or label contains directions for cooking, they should be followed. If you do not have such directions, use these:

1. Remove outside wrapper but do not remove rind.

2. Rewrap loosely in inside wrapper, Alcoa Wrap or waxed paper.

3. Place, fat side up, on rack in open roasting pan.

4. If using a meat thermometer, insert through paper into thickest part of meat, being sure bulb does not touch bone, gristle or fat.

5. Add no water.

6. Bake according to temperature-time chart.

7. About 45 minutes before baking time is completed, remove ham from oven; remove wrapper.

8. Remove rind with sharp knife or kitchen scissors.

9. Cut or score fat surface into squares or diamonds.

10. Stick whole cloves in center of each.

11. Glaze according to directions, To Glaze Baked Ham, page 78.

12. Return to 325° F. oven; bake 45 minutes longer or until nicely browned.

13. If desired, ham may be baked for complete time, then glazed and returned to 400° F. oven 15–20 minutes.

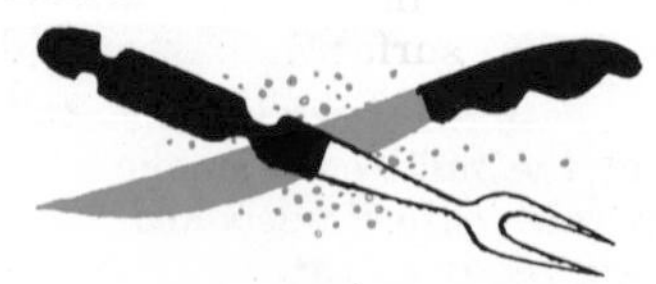

HAM Recipes

TO BAKE WHOLE OR HALF COOKED SMOKED HAMS WITH BONE IN OR BONE OUT

1. Remove wrapper.

2. Place on rack in open roasting pan.

3. Add no water; do not baste.

4. Bake 15–20 minutes per pound in slow oven 325° F. or if using meat thermometer, until it registers 130°F.

5. If desired, glaze according to directions, To Glaze Baked Ham, page 78.

TO BAKE OLD TYPE SMOKED HAM

These are the hams that are heavy cured, heavy smoked.

1. Soak overnight or for several hours in cold water to cover.

2. Drain; add fresh water to cover.

3. Cover; simmer until tender, allowing 25–30 minutes per pound.

4. Drain; remove skin; score fat and glaze according to directions, To Glaze Baked Ham, page 78.

VIRGINIA or KENTUCKY STYLE HAM

These hams have a special type of cure. Their surface is extremely dark and firm. They need special cooking to develop their fine flavor.

1. Scrub thoroughly with soapsuds and brush.

2. Wash well in hot water to remove all soap, using a knife to scrape off mold.

3. Soak 12–36 hours (depending on age) in cold water to cover; drain.

4. Place on rack in deep regular roaster.

5. Add warm water to cover ⅓ of ham.

6. Bake *uncovered* in moderate oven 350° F. allowing about 18 minutes per pound.

7. Turn once when ham is half done.

8. When done, tiny bone at end can be pulled out easily.

9. Allow to cool slightly; remove skin but use it as cover to keep ham moist.

10. Serve hot or cold; slice thin.

11. If desired, after scrubbing and soaking, ham may be simmered until tender allowing 30 minutes per pound. Then cool in cooking liquid, skin and glaze according to directions, To Glaze Baked Ham, page 78.

PANBROILED HAM SLICES

1. Snip outer edges of fat to prevent curling.

2. Brown in hot fry pan over moderate heat, turning once.

3. If slice is:

¼ in. thick, panbroil 5-6 min.
½ in. thick, panbroil 8-10 min.
¾ in. thick, panbroil 12-14 min.
1 in. thick, panbroil 15-16 min.

4. If slice is of precooked variety, reduce above times by 1–2 minutes.

HAM Recipes

TO GLAZE BAKED HAM

1. Cook ham according to recipe.
2. Remove rind; score or cut fat into squares or diamonds.
3. Insert whole clove into center of each diamond.
4. Spread or baste with one of the following:

¾ cup canned crushed pineapple and
¾ cup brown sugar
Pat brown sugar over ham; drizzle on honey or molasses

1 cup brown sugar mixed with juice and grated rind of 1 orange

1 cup currant jelly or canned whole cranberry sauce, beaten with fork

1 cup orange, or orange grapegruit marmalade, beaten with fork

1 cup brown sugar combined with 1 cup juice from spiced or pickled peaches

1 cup pureed applesauce, apricots or peaches

1 cup brown sugar mixed with 1 teaspoon dry mustard, 2 tablespoons vinegar, fruit juice or cider or 1 teaspoon horseradish

1 cup brown sugar combined with ¼ cup fine soft bread crumbs

Pat brown sugar over ham; place drained pineapple slices on top and maraschino cherry in center of each slice. Fruit may be fastened to ham with toothpicks and removed before serving. Use pineapple juice for basting.

Canned pineapple juice, cider, canned fruit nectar, corn syrup, maple syrup, muscatel or Tokay wine may be used for basting.

5. Complete baking as recipe directs or bake 15–20 minutes in moderate oven 400° F. until golden brown.

TO SIMMER UNCOOKED MILD CURE HAM

Bone-In Type

1. Cover whole or half with boiling water.
2. Add peeled clove of garlic, one stalk celery cut into 2 inch pieces.
3. Cover; simmer over low heat same number of minutes per pound shown in Baking Chart, page 75.
4. When tender, remove from liquid; remove rind; score fat; glaze according to directions, To Glaze Baked Ham.
5. Bake 15–20 minutes in moderate oven 400° F. or until brown.
6. If desired, cider or pineapple juice may be substituted for part of the boiling water.

Bone-Out Type

1. Simmer as directed for Bone-In Type.
2. Do not remove transparent casing until *after* ham is cooked.

HAM Recipes

TO SIMMER BONELESS SMOKED SHOULDER BUTT

1. Place 2–2½ pound smoked butt in large deep kettle.

2. Add boiling water to cover; 1 peeled clove of garlic, 6 whole cloves, 1 bay leaf, 4 peppercorns.

3. Cover, simmer over low heat 2 hours or until tender; drain.

4. Four servings.

BROILED HAM SLICES

2 center cut slices uncooked ham, ¾ inch thick

1. Trim excess fat, tough brown skin from meat; make several small gashes around edge of fat to prevent curling.

2. Spread top side with mustard.

3. Preheat broiler with pan in position 10 minutes; place meat on rack 3½ inches below heat.

4. Broil as follows:

Thickness of Slice	*Total Broiling Time*
½ inch	10–12 minutes (turn once)
¾ inch	15–17 minutes (turn once)
1 inch	20–22 minutes (turn once)

5. If ham is of *precooked* variety, broil about one half of time specified.

AMERICAN SPAGHETTI

1 tablespoon butter
1 large slice ham, cut into small pieces
½ cup minced onion
½ pound grated American cheese
2 cups canned tomatoes
½ cup water
¾ cup diced canned mushrooms
½ cup diced green pepper
1 8 ounce box spaghetti

1. Melt butter in heavy fry pan.

2. Add ham, onion; cook until lightly browned.

3. Remove from pan.

4. Add cheese to fat in pan; stir until dissolved.

5. Add tomatoes, water; mix thoroughly.

6. Add mushrooms, green pepper, ham-onion mixture.

7. Cover; simmer over low heat 10–15 minutes.

8. Boil spaghetti in salted water until tender; rinse; drain.

9. Pile spaghetti on large platter; top with ham mixture.

10. Serve with Parmesan cheese.

11. Six servings.

HAM *Recipes*

BAKED HAM SLICE

1. Place center cut slice of ham in shallow baking pan.

2. Cover with any of glazes listed under, To Glaze Baked Ham, page 78. or:

spread with prepared mustard; top with 2–3 tablespoons crushed corn flakes or

sprinkle with 2 tablespoons brown sugar, mixed with ⅛ teaspoon ground cloves or

spread with ½ cup currant jelly mixed with 2 tablespoons bottled horseradish

3. Pour 1 cup milk, water or fruit juice around ham.

4. Bake in moderate oven 325° F. until tender:

1½ inch slice from uncooked ham 1½ hours

2 inch slice from uncooked ham 2 hours

1–2 inch slice from cooked ham 15–20 minutes

5. Slices from uncooked ham should be covered during first 30 minutes of baking time.

HAM SHORTCAKE

¼ pound fresh mushrooms, sliced
3 tablespoons fat
¼ cup flour
1½ cups milk
¼ teaspoon salt
Pepper
1¼ cups diced cooked ham
¼ teaspoon bottled thick condiment sauce

1. Sauté mushrooms in fat in heavy fry pan until tender.

2. Stir in flour; add milk, salt, pepper.

3. Cook over low heat until thickened, stirring constantly.

4. Add ham.

5. Serve over squares of hot corn bread, baking powder biscuits, toast or in toast cups or patty shells.

6. Four servings.

HAM AND VEAL LOAF

1 pound smoked ham, ground
1 pound veal shoulder, ground
¼ cup quick cooking tapioca
1 teaspoon salt
⅛ teaspoon pepper
¼ cup minced onion
2 teaspoons Worcestershire Sauce
2 cups milk

1. Combine ingredients in order given.

2. Shape into loaf or pack into 9″ x 5″ x 3″ pan.

3. Bake 1½ hours in moderate oven 400° F.

4. Six servings.

HAM Recipes

STUFFED GREEN PEPPERS

- **6 large green peppers**
- **1 cup boiling water**
- **1½ teaspoons salt**
- **3 cups diced or coarsely ground cooked ham**
- **1½ cups cooked rice**
- **¼ teaspoon pepper**
- **¼ cup butter**
- **1 cup sliced onions**
- **4 peppercorns**
- **6 whole cloves**
- **1 cup condensed tomato soup, undiluted**
- **2½ cups canned tomatoes**

1. Wash peppers; cut thin slices from stem end; remove all seeds.

2. Cook peppers in boiling salted water in Dutch Oven 5 minutes.

3. Drain; reserve liquid.

4. Combine ham, rice, pepper.

5. Fill drained green peppers with this mixture.

6. Melt butter in Dutch Oven; add onion; sauté until golden brown.

7. Tie peppercorns, cloves in small piece of cheesecloth.

8. Add tomato soup, canned tomatoes, spice bag, liquid in which peppers were boiled to onions; mix.

9. Stand peppers upright in sauce.

10. Cover; simmer over low heat 30 minutes.

11. Six servings.

PINEAPPLE HAM LOAF

- **1½ pounds smoked ham, ground**
- **1 pound lean fresh pork, ground**
- **1 cup fine cracker crumbs**
- **2 eggs, slightly beaten**
- **1½ cups milk**
- **2 tablespoons prepared mustard**
- **½ cup brown sugar**
- **6 slices pineapple**
- **6 maraschino cherries**

1. Combine ham, pork, crumbs. eggs, milk, mustard.

2. Grease bottom, sides of heavy fry pan with butter.

3. Pat brown sugar on bottom.

4. Arrange pineapple slices on sugar.

5. Put cherry in center of each slice.

6. Pat meat mixture on top of pineapple.

7. Cover; place over low medium heat 10 minutes; reduce heat to low; cook 1 hour.

8. Remove from heat; tilt cover; drain off all liquid.

9. Place meat platter over loaf; invert ham; lift off.

10. Eight servings.

VARIETY MEAT RECIPES

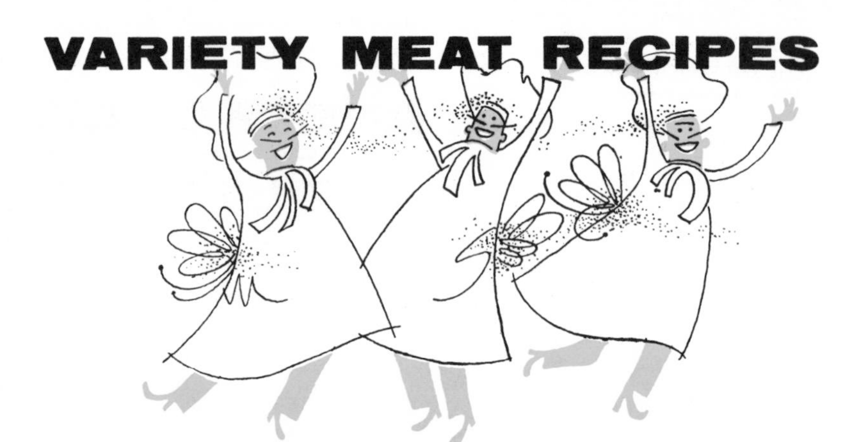

Brains, heart, liver, kidney, tongue, sweetbreads, and tripe are called variety meats. Since they are more perishable than other meats, they should be cooked within 24 hours of purchase.

SIMMERED BRAINS

1. Wash beef, veal, lamb or pork brains in cold water.

2. Soak ½ hour in salted water, allowing 1 tablespoon salt per quart water.

3. Remove membrane.

4. Place in pan; add water to cover, 1 teaspoon salt, 1 tablespoon lemon juice or vinegar for each quart water.

5. Cover; simmer over low heat 15–20 minutes.

6. Drain; drop into cold water; drain again.

7. Serve with Mushroom, Tomato or Butter Sauce.

8. Allow four servings per pound.

SAUTÉED BRAINS

1. Prepare Simmered Brains.

2. Dip into beaten egg, then in fine dry crumbs or corn meal.

3. Sauté in butter in fry pan until brown.

BROILED BRAINS

1. Prepare Simmered Brains.

2. Brush with melted butter.

3. Broil 10–15 minutes, turning occasionally.

4. Serve with lemon wedges, broiled bacon, broiled tomatoes or Beet and Horseradish Relish.

VARIETY MEAT Recipes

BEEF OR CALF HEART PATTIES

1½ pounds beef or calf heart, ground
1 medium onion, grated
1½ teaspoons salt
Pepper
3 tablespoons fat

1. Combine heart, onion, salt, pepper.
2. Shape into eight patties.
3. Melt fat in fry pan.
4. Add patties; cook slowly until browned on both sides—10 minutes.
5. Four servings.

BRAISED BEEF HEART

1 5 pound beef heart
3 tablespoons bacon drippings
1 cup sliced onions
6 cups boiling water
2 teaspoons salt
½ teaspoon pepper
1 teaspoon celery salt
2 teaspoons lemon juice

1. Remove fat, veins, arteries from cleaned heart.
2. Melt drippings in Dutch Oven; add onions; sauté uutil browned.
3. Add heart; brown on all sides.
4. Add water; salt, pepper, celery salt.
5. Cover; simmer 2½–3 hours or until tender.
6. Lift out meat; strain liquid.
7. Return 3 cups liquid to pan; add lemon juice.
8. Thicken for gravy.
9. Four servings.

STUFFED BEEF HEART

1. Follow recipe for Braised Beef Heart, filling with bread stuffing before cooking.

BROILED CALVES LIVER

8 slices liver, ½ inch thick
Salt
Pepper
4 tablespoons melted butter

1. Wipe liver with damp cloth; pat dry.
2. Sprinkle with salt, pepper; brush with melted butter.
3. Broil about 5 minutes each side; bacon strips may be broiled along with liver.
4. Four servings.

LIVER AND ONIONS

1. Roll slices of liver in seasoned flour.
2. Sauté in butter until brown on both sides.
3. Sauté thinly sliced onion rings in another fry pan until golden brown.
4. Place liver on platter; turn onion rings into pan in which liver was cooked. Add 2 tablespoons hot water; stir to loosen sediment in pan; mix; pour over liver.

VARIETY MEAT Recipes

BARBECUED BEEF LIVER

1 pound beef liver
Salt, pepper
1 cup sliced onions
2 tablespoons butter
1 tablespoon vinegar
1 tablespoon Worchestershire Sauce
1 teaspoon sugar
⅛ teaspoon pepper
1 teaspoon prepared mustard
⅛ teaspoon chili powder
¼ cup ketchup
1 tablespoon water

1. Cut liver into ¼ inch slices; cut each slice in half crosswise.
2. Arrange half the slices in bottom of covered baking pan.
3. Sprinkle lightly with salt, pepper.
4. Sauté onions until lightly browned in skillet; place half of them over liver.
5. Combine remaining ingredients.
6. Spoon half of sauce over liver-onion mixture.
7. Arrange another layer of liver and onions; cover pan.
8. Bake 25 minutes in moderate oven 325° F.
9. Uncover; pour remaining sauce over liver.
10. Bake uncovered 10 minutes.
11. Four servings.

LIVER PATTIES

1 pound ground beef, pork or lamb liver
1 onion, grated
1 teaspoon salt
⅛ teaspoon pepper
4 tablespoons fat

1. Combine liver, onion, salt, pepper; mix thoroughly; shape into 12 small patties.
2. Melt fat in fry pan.
3. Add patties; sauté over low heat until browned on both sides and cooked.
4. Four servings.

FRESH TONGUE

1 3–5 pound tongue
4 cups cold water
1½ teaspoons salt
½ cup diced celery
¼ cup chopped onion
½ cup sliced carrots
¼ cup vinegar
¼ cup sugar

1. Wash tongue; place in Dutch Oven; add remaining ingredients.
2. Cover; bring to boil; simmer over low heat until tender, allowing about 50 minutes per pound.
3. Let tongue cool in cooking liquid.
4. Remove skin; trim off thick end where small bones are apparent.
5. To serve cold: chill; slice thin.
6. To serve hot: reheat; serve with Horseradish Sauce, Barbecue Sauce, Spanish Sauce or Mustard Sauce.
7. Six servings.

VARIETY MEAT Recipes

SPICED TONGUE

1 4–5 pound smoked tongue
4 cups hot water
⅓ cup vinegar
2 teaspoons salt
3 tablespoons sugar
3 bay leaves
18 whole cloves
¾ cup sliced onion
1 tablespoon grated lemon rind

1. Soak tongue overnight in cold water; drain.
2. Place in Dutch Oven; add remaining ingredients.
3. Cover; bring to boil; simmer until tender, allowing about 50 minutes per pound.
4. Let tongue cool in cooking liquid.
5. Remove skin; trim thick end where small bones are apparent.
6. Serve as in Fresh Tongue.
7. Six servings.

BROILED KIDNEYS

1. Wash kidneys; split; remove fat, tubes with scissors.
2. Brush with melted butter or French Dressing.
3. Sprinkle with salt, pepper.
4. Broil 5–7 minutes on each side.
5. Serve on toast with melted butter to which a little lemon juice has been added.

BEEF KIDNEY STEW

1 beef kidney
6 cups boiling water
2 tablespoons minced onion
6 tablespoons flour
2 teaspoons salt
⅛ teaspoon pepper
⅛ teaspoon paprika
3 tablespoons butter
1 minced hard cooked egg

1. Cut kidney crosswise into ¼ inch slices.
2. Remove all fat, gristle; cut into small pieces.
3. Soak in cold water ½ hour; drain.
4. Add boiling water, onion; simmer uncovered 1 hour.
5. Cover; simmer ½ hour longer or until tender and only 3 cups liquid remain; cool.
6. Mix flour with 6 tablespoons cooled liquid to make paste.
7. Heat kidney mixture; add flour paste gradually, stirring constantly; cook until thickened.
8. Add salt, pepper, paprika, butter, egg.
9. Serve on toast or with hashed browned potatoes.
10. Four servings.

VARIETY MEAT Recipes

SWEETBREADS

1. Wash in cold water; let stand in cold water 20 minutes; drain.
2. Plunge into 2 quarts boiling water to which 2 tablespoons vinegar, 2 teaspoons salt have been added.
3. Cover; simmer 30 minutes.
4. Lift out, plunge again into cold water.
5. Drain; remove fat, connecting tissues, fine membrane; dry.
6. Split into halves lengthwise if very thick.
7. To serve, either broil or combine with Medium White Sauce. To broil:
   a. Brush with melted butter.
   b. Sprinkle with salt, pepper.
   c. Broil until golden brown, 5–7 minutes per side.
8. Serve on toast if broiled or in patty shells if creamed.
9. Medium White Sauce may be varied by adding 1½ teaspoons white wine, sherry or lemon juice with a little minced parsley.

TRIPE

1 pound fresh honeycomb tripe
Water to cover
½ teaspoon salt
1 egg, beaten
2 tablespoons water
Dry bread crumbs
4 tablespoons fat

1. Wash tripe; place in Dutch Oven or sauce pot; cover with water; add salt.
2. Cover; simmer over low heat 1 hour.
3. Drain; cut into serving pieces.
4. Combine egg, water.
5. Dip tripe into egg mixture, then into crumbs.
6. Sauté in melted fat until nicely browned on both sides.
7. Four servings.

POULTRY RECIPES

Temperature-Time Chart For Roasting Poultry

Drawn Weight Minus Head, Feet Organs	Oven Temperature	Approximate Number Minutes Per Pound
Chicken		
2–2¾ pounds	325° F.	66–63 minutes
2¾–3½ pounds	325° F.	55–51 minutes
3½–4½ pounds	325° F.	49–45 minutes
4½ pounds	325° F.	43 minutes
Capon		
6–7 pounds	325° F.	35 minutes
Turkey		
7–10 pounds	300° F.	30 minutes
10–15 pounds	300° F.	20 minutes
15–18 pounds	300° F.	18 minutes
18–20 pounds	300° F.	15 minutes
20–25 pounds	300° F.	13 minutes
Duck		
3–4¼ pounds	325°F.	45 minutes
4¼–5 pounds	325° F.	40 minutes
Goose		
7–8 pounds	325° F.	30 minutes
11 pounds	325° F.	25 minutes

POULTRY Recipes

TO DRAW POULTRY

1. Cut off head if not already done.

2. Remove pin feathers; use tweezers or catch pin feathers between thumb and paring knife.

3. Singe bird to remove hair—hold neck with one hand, feet with the other and turn bird over flame until all hair is removed.

4. Cut off oil sack at base of tail.

5. Remove feet—cut across front of leg joint, forcing shank down to dislocate joint; cut through skin at back of joint.

6. Remove tendons if necessary—tendons connect muscles of drumsticks with toes, seven in each leg. Make a cut 2 inches long at side of shank just beyond bone; insert a nutpick in opening; pull out tendons one at a time.

7. Remove neck—cut neck skin down center back to shoulder; free neck from neck skin; cut off neck at shoulder; set aside.

8. Remove gullet, crop, windpipe—pull these away from neck and skin; discard.

9. Remove entrails:

a. Cut skin of abdomen straight down from end of breastbone to within ½ inch of vent.

b. Insert forefinger into opening and bend finger around intestine leading to vent. Lift intestine up, then cut skin about ¾ inch around and completely encircling vent.

c. Insert hand, locate gizzard near center of cavity; pull out gizzard, heart, liver, intestines.

d. Cut away heart; remove attached heart sac; cut away blood vessels; squeeze to remove blood.

e. Lift liver from intestines; turn underside up to locate gall sac (a greenish brown sac holding bile); slip knife under sac to cut loose; cut away any part of liver stained by contact with it; do not break sac; if this should happen, discard any part of fowl on which it falls.

f. Cut out gizzard; cut into one side, cutting to but not into inner sac; pull gizzard away from sac; discard sac.

g. Insert hand high up into cavity and with fingers remove lungs (bright red spongy substance) from each side of backbone.

h. With fingers, loosen and remove all reddish brown substance clinging to backbone between ribs, fat and kidneys.

10. Scrub skin with brush or coarse cloth, using lukewarm water; rinse inside and outside first with warm then cold water; rinse giblets; drain. Pat carcass and giblets dry with towel.

POULTRY Recipes

TO DISJOINT or CUT UP CHICKEN

1. Cut off Wings: grasp wings, bending back away from body; cut through skin, flesh, joint.

2. Cut off Legs: hold legs away from body; cut skin from leg joint near backbone around to and near tail; sever leg joint near backbone. Cut through remaining skin on back to free leg completely; divide leg into thigh and drumstick.

3. Separate Back and Breast: lay carcass on side; cut through flesh in straight line from abdominal opening through ribs to where wings were removed; turn bird over, make same cut to second wing. Hold tail and with other hand grasp tip of breast, lifting it up and away from back. Pull back until shoulder joints break, separating breast from back. Separate breast and back into 2 or 3 pieces.

ROAST DUCK

1 4–5 pound drawn duck
½ teaspoon salt
4 cups bread crumbs
¼ cup minced onion
¼ cup minced green pepper
½ cup minced celery
1 teaspoon salt
⅛ teaspoon pepper
1 tablespoon sage

1. Wash, clean, dry duck.

2. Rub inside with salt.

3. Combine remaining ingredients to make stuffing.

4. Stuff cavity, neck; tie legs together.

5. Place breast side up on rack in open roasting pan.

6. Do not grease; add no water; do not cover.

7. Roast according to Temperature-Time Chart, page 87; these times are approximate; differences in ducks may necessitate increasing or decreasing time.

8. Do not prick skin with fork; this allows juices to escape.

9. If duck is very fat, remove excess fat from pan during roasting.

10. Four servings.

Variations

1. Instead of stuffing duck, place 1 quartered apple, 1 quartered onion, 2 stalks celery in cavity; remove after roasting.

2. Five minutes before roasting time is completed, pour Orange Sauce, page 106, over duck.

POULTRY Recipes

ROAST GOOSE

1. Clean, wash, dry goose.

2. Rub cavity with salt, allowing ⅛ teaspoon salt per pound.

3. To reduce fat: place goose on rack in open roasting pan, in moderately hot oven 375° F., 15–20 minutes or until fat runs; dip out fat; repeat until fat ceases to drip; then stuff.

4. Stuff with Celery Stuffing, page 101, Apple Raisin Stuffing, page 100, or place 1 quartered apple, 1 peeled onion, 2 stalks celery in cavity; remove after roasting.

5. Prick fat on back, around tail and skin around wings and legs with fork.

6. Place stuffed goose, breast side up, on rack in open roasting pan.

7. Add no water; do not grease; do not cover.

8. Roast according to Temperature-Time Chart, page 87; these times are approximate. Differences in birds may necessitate increasing or decreasing time.

9. To test for doneness, grasp end of leg bone. If thigh joint moves easily, goose is done. Drumstick meat will also be very soft when pressed with finger.

10. If goose is very fat, remove excess fat from pan during roasting.

ROAST TURKEY

1. Prepare, stuff, truss turkey as for Roast Stuffed Chicken, page 92.

2. Grease turkey thoroughly with soft butter; sprinkle with salt, pepper.

3. Place breast side down in V type rack or lay breast side up on rack in open roasting pan.

4. Place piece of Alcoa Wrap tent fashion over top of turkey, allowing it to remain loose so heat can circulate around under it.

5. Add no water; do not cover; do not baste.

6. Roast according to Temperature-Time Chart, page 87; these times are approximate; differences in turkeys may necessitate increasing or decreasing time.

7. To test for doneness, grasp end of leg bone. If thigh joint moves easily, bird is done. Also, drumstick meat should be very soft when pressed with finger. Do not pierce with fork.

8. When done, remove skewers, pins, cord from turkey.

9. Make gravy from juices in pan.

10. If turkey is allowed to set 5 minutes after removal from oven, it will be easier to carve.

11. Allow ½-¾ pound per person.

POULTRY Recipes

ROAST HALF TURKEY

1. Wash, clean turkey.
2. Rub inside with salt, 1/8 teaspoon per pound.
3. Fasten skin to breast meat on keel bone edge to prevent shrinkage of skin.
4. Tie leg to tail; leave wing flat against breast.
5. Place turkey, cut side down, on rack in uncovered open roasting pan.
6. Brush bird with melted fat.
7. Place piece of Alcoa Wrap tent fashion over top of turkey allowing it to remain loose so heat can circulate around under it.
8. Add no water; do not cover; do not baste.
9. Roast 25-30 minutes per pound in moderate oven 325° F.
10. Prepare Bread Stuffing, page 101.
11. When bird is half done, remove from rack.
12. Cut a double thick piece of Alcoa Wrap into an oval about the size of turkey.
13. Grease; lay on roaster rack; make mound of stuffing.
14. Place turkey, skin side up, over stuffing.
15. Return to oven: complete roasting.
16. Additional stuffing may be baked in Alcoa Wrap or in covered baking pan.

ROAST CAPON

1. Prepare, stuff, truss capon as for Roast Stuffed Chicken, page 92.
2. Grease thoroughly with soft butter; sprinkle with salt, pepper.
3. Place breast side down in V type rack or lay breast side up on rack in open roasting pan.
4. Place piece of Alcoa Wrap tent fashion over top of capon, allowing it to remain loose so heat can circulate around under it.
5. Add no water; do not cover; do not baste.
6. Roast according to Temperature-Time Chart, page 87.
7. To test for doneness, grasp end of leg bone. If thigh joint moves easily, bird is done. Also, drumstick meat should be very soft when pressed with finger. Do not pierce meat with fork.
8. When done, remove skewers, pins, cord from capon.
9. Make gravy from juices in pan.
10. If capon is allowed to set 5 minutes after removing from oven, it will be easier to carve.
11. Allow 1/2-3/4 pound per person.

POULTRY Recipes

ROAST STUFFED CHICKEN

1. Wash, clean chicken; dry thoroughly.

2. Rub inside with salt, about ⅛ teaspoon per pound.

3. Fill cavity, neck opening with desired stuffing; pack lightly.

4. Close cavity with skewers or poultry pins, laced with cord; pull neck skin back over stuffing; fasten with skewers or poultry pins to back of bird.

5. Using long cord, tie ends of legs together; bring cord from legs down around tail, drawing legs down close to body; tie legs to tail.

6. Bend tip ends of wings backward so they are held against back of bird.

7. Grease bird thoroughly with soft butter; sprinkle with salt, pepper.

8. Place bird breast side down in V type rack or lay breast side up on rack in open roasting pan.

9. Place piece of Alcoa Wrap, tent fashion over chicken, allowing it to remain loose so heat can circulate around under it.

10. Add no water; do not cover; do not baste.

11. Roast according to temperature-time chart; these times are approximate; difference in birds may necessitate increasing or decreasing time.

12. To test for doneness, grasp end of leg bone; if thigh joint moves easily, bird is done; meat on drumsticks will be very soft when pressed with finger; never pierce with fork.

13. When bird is done, remove skewers, pins, cord.

15. Make gravy from juices in pan.

16. If chicken is allowed to set 5 minutes after removing from oven, it will be easier to carve.

17. Allow ½–¾ pound per person.

BROILED CHICKEN

1. Preheat broiler—with broiler pan in position 10 minutes or as manufacturer directs.

2. Wash, clean, split 1¼–2 pound young chicken.

3. Place on broiler rack 3–3½ inches from heat, skin side down.

4. Brush well with melted butter or other fat.

5. Broil slowly so chicken just begins to brown at end of 10–12 minutes.

6. Turn; brush with melted butter every 10 minutes as browning increases.

7. Broil until tender and evenly browned—about 30–45 minutes, depending upon size.

8. Chicken is done when meat of drumstick is tender and it has lost all pink color.

9. Chicken may be served in halves if small, or in quarters if larger.

POULTRY Recipes

BROILED SQUAB

1. Clean, wash, dry, split squab.
2. Season with salt, pepper.
3. Broil as in Broiled Chicken, page 92, until tender, about 30–45 minutes.
4. Allow 1 squab per person.

SOUTHERN FRIED CHICKEN

1. Wash; clean chicken; cut into desired serving pieces.
2. For each pound of chicken, combine 2 tablespoons corn meal, 2 tablespoons flour, ½ teaspoon salt, ⅛ teaspoon pepper, 1 teaspoon paprika in paper bag.
3. Add chicken; shake until pieces are thoroughly coated.
4. Brown thoroughly on all sides in melted fat in heavy fry pan or Dutch Oven.
5. Cover; cook over low heat 35–60 minutes or until tender.

FRIED CHICKEN NO. 1

1. For each pound of chicken combine ¼ cup flour, ½ teaspoon salt, ⅛ teaspoon pepper, 1 teaspoon paprika; put into paper bag.
2. Wash, dry chicken; cut into desired size pieces.
3. Drop into bag; shake until chicken is coated with flour.
4. Melt fat (part butter, part shortening or cooking oil) to depth of ¼ inch in 2 heavy fry pans.
5. Put meaty pieces into 1 pan; boney pieces into the other.
6. Fry slowly, turning frequently until golden brown.
7. Cover; cook over low heat until tender, 35–60 minutes, depending upon size of chicken.
8. When almost tender, remove cover.
9. Lift out chicken; make gravy from drippings.

FRIED CHICKEN NO. 2

1. Wash, dry chicken; rub skin lightly with cut side of clove of garlic.
2. Cut chicken into desired serving pieces.
3. Coat each piece with flour combined with salt, pepper.
4. Brown thoroughly on all sides in fat (part butter, part shortening) in heavy fry pan.
5. Sprinkle all pieces generously with paprika.
6. Add 1 cup boiling water.
7. Cover; cook over low heat 30–60 minutes or until tender.

POULTRY Recipes

OVEN FRIED CHICKEN NO. 1

1. Wash; dry chicken; cut into desired size serving pieces.
2. Combine ½ cup flour, 1 teaspoon salt, ½ teaspoon ginger; place in paper bag.
3. Add chicken; shake until each piece is thoroughly coated.
4. Place chicken in shallow baking pan.
5. Melt ¼ pound butter, ½ cup shortening in sauce pan.
6. Spoon some of butter mixture over chicken.
7. Place in moderate oven 350° F.
8. Bake about 1 hour or until meat is tender, basting every 10 minutes with more of the butter mixture.

OVEN FRIED CHICKEN NO. 2

1. Wash; dry chicken; coat thoroughly with seasoned flour.
2. Brown on all sides in fat in fry pan.
3. Place chicken in covered baking pan, casserole or roasting pan.
4. Cover; bake 1 hour or until tender in moderate oven 350° F. Uncover last 10 minutes.

FRENCH FRIED CHICKEN

1 3 pound young chicken
1 cup boiling water
2 stalks celery, diced
1 carrot, sliced
1 small onion, sliced
2 sprigs parsley
1 teaspoon salt
2 cups all purpose flour
3 teaspoons baking powder
½ teaspoon salt
2 eggs, beaten
1½ cups milk

1. Wash; clean chicken; cut into desired serving pieces.
2. Place in sauce pot; add water, celery, carrots, onion, parsley, salt.
3. Cover; simmer 30–45 minutes until tender.
4. Allow to cool in liquid; remove; dry each piece thoroughly with towel.
5. To make batter; sift flour, baking powder, salt together; combine eggs, milk; add liquid to dry ingredients; beat until smooth.
6. Dip each piece of chicken into batter.
7. Melt 1 pound fat in Dutch Oven or French fryer; heat to 375° F.
8. Drop chicken into fat, cooking until golden brown; do only 2–3 pieces at a time.

POULTRY Recipes

MARYLAND FRIED CHICKEN

- 1 2½–3 pound young chicken
- ¾ teaspoon salt
- ½ teaspoon pepper
- ¾ cup dry crumbs
- 1 egg, well beaten
- 2 tablespoons milk
- ½ cup shortening
- 2 tablespoons flour
- ½ teaspoon salt
- ⅛ teaspoon pepper
- 1 cup milk

1. Wash; clean; cut up chicken.
2. Mix salt, pepper, crumbs.
3. Dip chicken into egg combined with milk, then into crumbs.
4. Melt shortening in heavy fry pan or Dutch Oven.
5. Add chicken; brown thoroughly on all sides.
6. Cover; reduce heat to low.
7. Cook 45–60 minutes or until chicken is tender; if chicken becomes dry, add a little water.
8. Remove chicken from pan.
9. Add flour, salt, pepper to liquid in pan; stir; add milk.
10. Cook over low heat, stirring constantly until thickened.
11. Four servings.

CHICKEN CACCIATORE

- 1 3½ pound chicken
- ½ cup fat
- 1 onion, sliced
- 2½ cups canned tomatoes
- ½ teaspoon salt
- ⅛ teaspoon pepper

1. Wash, clean chicken; cut into serving pieces.
2. Brown on all sides in melted fat in Dutch Oven.
3. Add onion, tomatoes, salt, pepper.
4. Cover; reduce heat to low.
5. Cook 45–50 minutes or until chicken is tender.
6. Serve with spaghetti.
7. Six servings.

CHICKEN 'N DUMPLINGS

- 1 5–6 pound stewing chicken
- 3 cups water
- 1 sliced carrot
- 1 small onion, sliced
- 2 stalks celery, cut

1. Wash, clean chicken; cut into desired serving pieces.
2. Place water in large sauce pot or Dutch Oven.
3. Add carrot, onion, celery; bring to boil.
4. Add chicken; bring to boil.
5. Cover; reduce heat to low.
6. Simmer 2–2½ hours or until tender.
7. Remove chicken; strain liquid; add milk, cream or water to make 2 cups.
8. Return chicken to pot.
9. Prepare drop dumplings as in Veal Stew With Dumplings, page 58.
10. Drop on top of chicken.
11. Cover; cook 12–15 minutes; do not remove cover until end of cooking time.
12. Six servings.

POULTRY Recipes

MAGGIE'S CHICKEN MORNAY

Part One:

- **4 breasts of chicken**
- **½ cup flour**
- **1 teaspoon salt**
- **⅛ teaspoon pepper**
- **⅛ teaspoon ginger**
- **½ cup butter**
- **1 cup water**

Part Two:

- **4 tablespoons butter**
- **4 tablespoons flour**
- **1 teaspoon salt**
- **½ cup cream**
- **½ cup milk**
- **1 cup liquid from fry pan**
- **½ cup grated American cheese**
- **1 cup diced canned mushrooms**
- **½ cup grated American cheese**

Part One:

1. Coat chicken breasts with flour combined with salt, pepper, ginger.
2. Brown on all sides in butter in heavy fry pan.
3. Cover; cook over low heat 30–45 minutes or until tender; a little water may be added if necessary.
4. Place breasts in shallow baking pan.
5. Add water to drippings in pan; stir to loosen any sediment in pan.

Part Two:

1. Melt butter in sauce pan; remove from heat.
2. Add flour, salt; blend thoroughly.
3. Add cream; blend.
4. Add milk, liquid from fry pan.
5. Return to low heat; cook, stirring constantly until thickened.
6. Add cheese; stir until melted.
7. Add mushrooms.
8. Pour sauce over chicken.
9. Sprinkle grated cheese over top.
10. Bake 25–30 minutes in moderate oven 350° F. until cheese is melted and just lightly browned.
11. Sprinkle with paprika; serve at once.
12. Four servings.

CHICKEN FRICASSEE

- **1 4½-5 pound chicken**
- **½ cup flour**
- **2 teaspoons salt**
- **⅛ teaspoon pepper**
- **4 tablespoons fat**
- **4 cups boiling water**
- **1 large onion, peeled, quartered**
- **Few celery tops**
- **1 teaspoon salt**

1. Wash, clean chicken; cut into desired pieces.
2. Combine flour, salt, pepper in paper bag.
3. Add chicken; shake until coated.
4. Melt fat in Dutch Oven.
5. Add chicken; brown thoroughly on all sides.
6. Add water, onion, celery tops, salt.
7. Cover; simmer over low heat until tender; allow about 1–1½ hours for roaster, 3–4 hours for older fowl; add more water if necessary.
8. Remove chicken; thicken gravy.
9. Six servings.

POULTRY Recipes

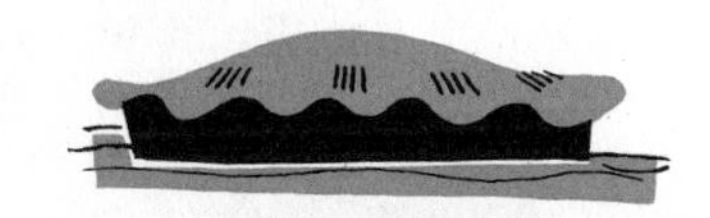

CHICKEN PIE

1 4-pound chicken
Boiling water
1 tablespoon salt
2 stalks celery
1 bay leaf
1 medium onion, sliced
3 cups cooked diced potatoes
2 cups cooked diced carrots
1 cup cooked or canned peas
7 tablespoons butter and fat from chicken
7 tablespoons flour
1 teaspoon salt
⅛ teaspoon pepper
1 cup milk or cream
2 cups chicken broth
Dash nutmeg
½ teaspoon Worcestershire Sauce
Pinch tarragon

1. Wash, clean chicken.

2. Place in Dutch Oven or sauce pot.

3. Add boiling water to cover chicken half way.

4. Add salt, celery, bay leaf, onion.

5. Cover; simmer until tender; allow 1–1½ hours for roaster; 3–4 hours for older fowl; additional water may be added if necessary.

6. Remove chicken; allow to cool.

7. Strain broth; add water to make 2 cups; skim off fat as it cools.

8. Remove skin from chicken; cut meat into 1 inch cubes.

9. Arrange chicken, potatoes, carrots, peas in casserole or shallow baking pan.

10. Melt fat in sauce pan; remove from heat.

11. Stir in flour, salt, pepper.

12. Add milk, chicken broth, nutmeg, Worcestershire Sauce, tarragon.

13. Cook over low heat, stirring constantly until thickened.

14. Pour over chicken-vegetable mixture.

15. Top with baking powder biscuits or flaky pie crust.

16. Brush with milk.

17. Bake 20–25 minutes in hot oven 425° F.

18. Six servings.

Variations

1. Leftover chicken may be used.

2. Part chicken, part ham may be used.

3. Heap fluffy mashed white or sweet potatoes on top instead of biscuits or pie crust.

CREAMED CHICKEN

1 4-pound chicken
⅓ cup butter or chicken fat
⅓ cup flour
1 cup chicken broth
1½ cups milk or cream

1. Prepare chicken as for Chicken Pie.

2. Melt butter in top of double boiler; remove from heat.

3. Stir in flour; add broth, milk.

4. Cook over low heat, stirring constantly until thickened.

5. Add salt, pepper, if necessary.

6. Add diced chicken; place over boiling water until chicken is hot.

7. Serve on toast, waffles, rice, noodles, biscuits or split hot corn bread.

8. Six servings.

POULTRY Recipes

CHICKEN A LA KING

Prepare Creamed Chicken, page 97; add ½ pound sautéed sliced fresh mushrooms, 1 pimento cut into strips and a little sherry to taste.

CREAMED CHICKEN SUPREME

Prepare Creamed Chicken, page 97. Place slices of toast in shallow baking pan; pile 3–4 tablespoons Creamed Chicken on each slice; top with slice sharp American cheese. Slide under broiler until cheese melts; sprinkle with paprika and crumbled cooked bacon.

CHICKEN PAPRIKA

1 2½-3 pound chicken
3 tablespoons butter
1 cup chopped onion
2 teaspoons paprika
2 chicken bouillon cubes
2 cups boiling water
1 teaspoon salt
1 teaspoon flour
1 cup sour cream

1. Wash, clean chicken; cut into desired serving pieces.

2. Melt butter in Dutch Oven.

3. Add onions; sauté until browned.

4. Add paprika, bouillon cubes dissolved in boiling water; salt.

5. Bring to boil; add chicken.

6. Cover; cook over low heat about 1 hour or until chicken is tender.

7. Stir flour into sour cream.

8. Pour slowly into liquid in pot; stir; spoon over chicken.

9. Cover; cook five minutes longer.

10. Four servings.

CHICKEN CHOW MEIN

2 cups cubed cooked chicken
2 tablespoons butter
2 cups thinly sliced celery
1½ cups sliced peeled onions
⅛ teaspoon pepper
2 cups chicken broth
1 No. 2 can mixed Chinese vegetables
½ cup canned mushroom caps
2 tablespoons cornstarch
3 tablespoons soy sauce
1 5-ounce can fried noodles

1. Brown chicken lightly in butter in fry pan or Dutch Oven.

2. Add celery, onions, pepper, broth.

3. Cover; cook until vegetables are tender.

4. Add drained Chinese vegetables, mushrooms; bring to boil.

5. Mix cornstarch to soy sauce; add to hot mixture, stirring constantly.

6. Simmer 2 minutes or until slightly thickened.

7. Place on deep platter; top with noodles.

8. Six servings.

POULTRY Recipes

CREOLE CHICKEN

- **1 3½-pound chicken**
- **1 clove garlic**
- **6 slices bacon**
- **½ pound ham, diced**
- **2 small onions, chopped**
- **2 cups drained canned tomatoes**
- **1 tablespoon chopped parsley**
- **⅛ teaspoon Tabasco Sauce**
- **½ teaspoon thyme**
- **2 teaspoons salt**
- **2 cups boiling water**
- **2 cups cooked sliced okra**

1. Wash; clean chicken; cut into desired serving pieces.
2. Rub skin side of each piece with cut side of clove of garlic.
3. Place bacon in cold Dutch Oven or heavy fry pan; cook until crisp; remove; crumble.
4. Add chicken; brown on all sides; remove.
5. Add ham, onions; brown lightly.
6. Add bacon, chicken, tomatoes, parsley, Tabasco Sauce, thyme, salt, water.
7. Cover; reduce heat to low.
8. Cook 30–60 minutes or until chicken is tender.
9. Add okra last 10 minutes.
10. Thicken gravy if desired.
11. Eight servings.

CHICKEN LIVERS SAUTÉ

- **1 pound chicken livers**
- **¼ cup butter**
- **¼ cup flour**
- **2 cups hot water**
- **1 teaspoon salt**
- **2 teaspoons bottled thick meat sauce**

1. Clean; cut livers into halves.
2. Sauté in butter in fry pan over low heat until lightly browned; remove livers.
3. Add flour; stir; add water; cook, stirring constantly until thickened.
4. Add salt, meat sauce, livers.
5. Serve on toast or over cooked rice or with omelet.

Variations

1. Mushrooms may be sautéed along with livers.
2. Few slices green peppers or minced onion may be cooked with livers.
3. Use curry powder to taste instead of bottled meat sauce.

POULTRY Recipes

CROQUETTES

Croquettes are an ideal way to utilize leftover meat or fowl.

CROQUETTES

4 tablespoons butter
4 tablespoons flour
½ teaspoon salt
⅛ teaspoon pepper
1 cup milk
2 teaspoons minced parsley
2 cups ground cooked meat or poultry
1 teaspoon lemon juice
1 teaspoon minced onion
1 egg, beaten
1 tablespoon water
Fine bread or cracker crumbs
Fat or oil

1. Melt butter in sauce pan; remove from heat.
2. Add flour, salt, pepper; blend; add milk.
3. Cook over low heat, stirring constantly until thickened.
4. Add parsley, meat, lemon juice, onion; chill thoroughly.
5. Divide mixture into 8 portions; shape into rolls or balls.
6. Combine egg, water.
7. Roll croquettes in crumbs, then egg mixture, then crumbs; chill again.
8. Heat fat in French fryer to 390° F. or until hot enough to brown an inch cube of bread in 20 seconds.
9. Fry only a few croquettes at a time; place in basket; lower in fat; cook until golden brown—about 2 minutes.
10. Lift basket; allow food to drain a few seconds, then place on absorbent paper or cake cooling rack.
11. Serve plain or with Spanish, Mushroom, Tomato or Horseradish Sauce.
12. Yield: 8 croquettes.

Variations

1. Cooked rice may be substituted for part of meat.
2. Cooked finely diced vegetables may be substituted for part of meat.
3. Form croquette mixture into patties; brown on both sides in small amount of fat in fry pan.
4. Prepare croquette mixture; pour into shallow baking pan to depth of 1 inch; chill; cut into 2–3 inch squares; dip in crumbs, egg, then crumbs again. These are sometimes called cutlets.
5. Serve with white sauce to which a few cooked peas, mushrooms have been added.

STUFFING

APPLE RAISIN STUFFING

1 cup minced onion
3 cups diced pared, cored apples
1 cup seedless raisins
1½ teaspoons salt
7½ cups day-old bread crumbs
⅛ teaspoon pepper
3 tablespoons granulated sugar
¾ cup melted butter

1. Combine all ingredients.
2. Sufficient stuffing for a 10 pound goose.

POULTRY Recipes

BREAD STUFFING

½ cup butter
¼ cup minced onion
¼ cup diced celery
16 slices bread
¾ teaspoon salt
½ teaspoon poultry seasoning
1 tablespoon minced parsley
⅛ teaspoon pepper

1. Melt butter in large fry pan; add onion, celery; sauté until tender.
2. Cut crusts from bread; toast bread.
3. Dip bread into milk, then squeeze out; crumble into butter mixture.
4. Add salt, poultry seasoning, parsley, pepper; stir until mixed.
5. Cook over low heat 3 minutes, stirring frequently; cool.
6. Sufficient stuffing for a 4 pound fowl.

CELERY STUFFING

6 cups finely diced celery
3 cups boiling water
¾ cup minced onion
¾ cup butter
3 teaspoons poultry seasoning
4 teaspoons salt
1 teaspoon pepper
6 quarts day-old bread cubes

1. Simmer celery in boiling water 15–20 minutes or until tender; drain, reserving 1 cup of liquid.
2. Sauté onion in butter over low heat until tender.
3. Combine seasonings, crumbs; add celery, the 1 cup celery liquid, onion-butter mixture.
4. Blend thoroughly.
5. Sufficient stuffing for a 15 pound turkey.

CHESTNUT STUFFING

½ pound chestnuts
1 tablespoon butter
½ pound sausage meat
¼ cup minced onion
½ cup hot water
1 teaspoon dried sage
1½ teaspoons salt
⅛ teaspoon pepper
2 cups soft bread cubes

1. Wash chestnuts; make long slit through shell on both sides.
2. Bake 15 minutes in hot oven 500° F.
3. Remove shells; skin; boil in salted water 20 minutes; drain; chop fine.
4. Melt butter; add sausage, onion; saute until sausage is cooked.
5. Add remaining ingredients, chestnuts; toss together lightly.
6. Sufficient stuffing for a 4 pound fowl.

OYSTER STUFFING

1 cup stewing oysters, chopped
4 cups stale bread cubes
2 teaspoons salt
⅛ teaspoon pepper
⅛ teaspoon sage
3 tablespoons butter
1 onion, minced
2 tablespoons minced parsley
¾ cup minced celery

1. Place chopped oysters in fry pan; cover; sauté 5 minutes; drain.
2. Combine bread cubes, salt, pepper, sage; add oysters.
3. Melt butter in fry pan; add onion, parsley, celery.
4. Sauté until tender; add to bread mixture; blend.
5. Sufficient stuffing for a 4 pound fowl.

SAUCE RECIPES for MEAT and POULTRY

SUPER BARBECUE SAUCE

1 large onion, sliced
2 tablespoons butter
1 cup canned tomatoes
1 cup diced celery
1 cup diced green pepper
1 cup ketchup
2 tablespoons brown sugar
3 dashes Tabasco Sauce
½ teaspoon dry mustard
2 cups beef stock or 2 bouillon cubes dissolved in 2 cups boiling water
1 teaspoon salt
⅛ teaspoon pepper

1. Brown onion in butter in Dutch Oven.
2. Add remaining ingredients; cover; bring to boil.
3. Simmer over low heat 1 hour.
4. Yield: approximately 3 cups sauce.
5. Serve with hamburgers, ribs, fried chicken.

MUSTARD SAUCE

1 tablespoon butter
2 tablespoons prepared mustard
2 teaspoons salt
2 teaspoons sugar
1 egg yolk, slightly beaten
1¼ cups cold water
5 teaspoons cornstarch
2 tablespoons cold water
1 tablespoon lemon juice

1. Melt butter in top of double boiler.
2. Stir in mustard, salt, sugar.
3. Combine egg yolk, water; stir into butter mixture.
4. Mix remaining cold water, cornstarch to a smooth paste.
5. Stir into sauce; cook over boiling water until thickened.
6. Remove from heat; add lemon juice.
7. Yield: approximately 1 cup sauce.

SAUCE Recipes

TOMATO SAUCE

2 cups canned tomatoes
1 sliced onion
2 stalks celery with leaves, chopped
1 tablespoon minced parsley
1 carrot, diced
½ green pepper, diced
3 tablespoons butter
3 tablespoons flour
¼ teaspoon salt
⅛ teaspoon pepper
¼ teaspoon sugar

1. Combine tomatoes, onion, celery, parsley, carrot, green pepper in sauce pan.

2. Cover; bring to boil; simmer 15 minutes; strain, reserving liquid.

3. Melt butter in sauce pan; remove from heat.

4. Add flour, salt, pepper, sugar; blend.

5. Add sufficient water, if necessary, to vegetable liquid to make 1½ cups.

6. Add to flour mixture; cook over low heat until bubbly, stirring constantly.

7. Yield: approximately 1½ cups sauce.

8. Serve over meat.

PERFECT GRAVY

¼ cup fat and drippings
¼ cup flour
2 cups liquid (juice from pan plus water)
Salt

1. When roast is done remove to heated platter; set in warm place while making gravy.

2. Remove ¼ cup fat and drippings from pan; pour into sauce pan; set aside.

3. Pour remaining drippings into a measuring cup.

4. Now pour enough warm water into roasting pan to make 2 cups of liquid, including what you have already measured, but not counting the ¼ cup. For example, if after removing the ¼ cup you have ½ cup left, you will pour 1½ cups water into roast pan.

5. Place over high heat; stir until sediment sticking to bottom of pan has become loosened; remove from heat; set aside.

6. Add flour to drippings in sauce pan; add about ½ cup of liquid; stir; add remaining liquid. *Now* place over heat; cook until thickened and bubbly, stirring constantly.

7. Remove from heat; add seasoning. If desired a few drops of thick condiment sauce may be added for color and flavor.

8. When you first start to cook the gravy, it will be lumpy but as it heats and you stir, the lumps will disappear. When finished the gravy will be as smooth as satin.

SAUCE Recipes

STEAK SAUCE

3 tablespoons butter
3 tablespoons lemon juice
½ teaspoon dry mustard
1 tablespoon Worcestershire Sauce
Salt
Pepper

1. Melt butter; add remaining ingredients.
2. Yield: ¼ cup sauce.
3. Serve with broiled meat.

BROWN GRAVY

1. Remove meat from pan; remove pan from heat.
2. Pour juice in pan into measuring cup.
3. Return 3 tablespoons of it to pan.
4. Add sufficient water to juice in cup to make 1 cup.
5. Add 2 tablespoons flour to juice in pan; blend.
6. Add liquid in cup; return to heat; cook slowly, stirring constantly until thickened and bubbly.
7. Add salt, pepper to taste.

GIBLET GRAVY

1. Simmer heart, liver, gizzard, neck, wing tips of fowl in 2½ cups salted water 30 minutes.
2. Remove giblets; chop fine; discard other pieces.
3. Melt 4 tablespoons fat in fry pan; add 4 tablespoons flour; blend.
4. Slowly add 2 cups stock from giblets; cook, stirring constantly until thickened; add chopped giblets.
5. Season to taste.

NUMBER TWO WHITE SAUCE

2 tablespoons butter
2 tablespoons flour
¼ teaspoon salt
1 cup milk

1. Melt butter in sauce pan; remove from heat.
2. Add flour, salt; stir; add milk.
3. Cook over low heat, stirring constantly until thickened.
4. Yield: 1 cup sauce.

NUMBER THREE WHITE SAUCE

3 tablespoons butter
3 tablespoons flour
¼ teaspoon salt
1 cup milk

1. Melt butter in sauce pan; remove from heat.
2. Add flour, salt; stir; add milk.
3. Cook over low heat, stirring constantly until thickened.
4. Yield: 1 cup sauce.

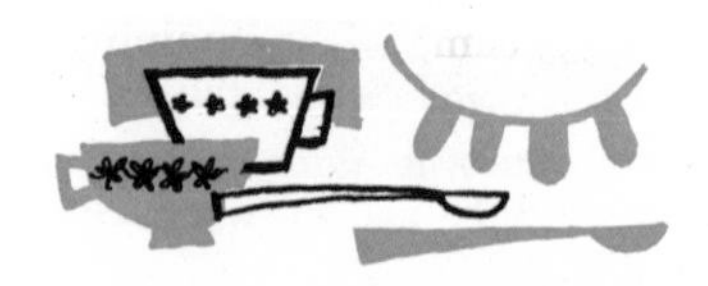

SAUCE Recipes

CHEESE SAUCE

1 cup grated American cheese
1 cup No. 2 White Sauce

1. Add cheese to white sauce; stir until cheese melts.
2. Serve over chicken croquettes.

RAISIN SAUCE

½ cup brown sugar, firmly packed
1½ teaspoons dry mustard
1½ tablespoons flour
½ cup seedless raisins
¼ cup vinegar
1¾ cups water

1. Combine dry ingredients in top of double boiler; add vinegar, water.
2. Cook 20 minutes over boiling water.
3. Yield: approximately 2 cups sauce.
4. Serve over ham or fresh pork.

HORSERADISH SAUCE

1 cup whipping cream
1 tablespoon lemon juice
1½ tablespoons bottled horseradish
⅛ teaspoon salt

1. Whip cream; add remaining ingredients; blend thoroughly.
2. Yield: approximately 2½ cups sauce.
3. Serve with ham.

EGG SAUCE

2 hard cooked eggs, chopped
1 tablespoon capers or chopped sweet pickle
1 cup No. 2 White Sauce

1. Add eggs, capers or chopped pickle to white sauce; blend.
2. Serve over croquettes.

DRAWN BUTTER SAUCE

¼ cup butter
2 tablespoons chopped parsley
Salt
Paprika

1. Melt butter; add remaining ingredients.
2. Yield: ¼ cup sauce.

MINT SAUCE

½ cup vinegar
1 cup water
¼ cup chopped fresh mint leaves
¼ cup lemon juice
½ cup water
2 tablespoons sugar
¼ teaspoon salt
¼ cup chopped mint leaves

1. Combine vinegar, water, mint leaves; simmer until liquid is reduced one half; strain.
2. Add lemon juice, water, sugar, salt; stir; chill.
3. Just before serving add remaining crushed mint.
4. Yield: approximately 1 cup sauce.
5. Serve with cold roast lamb.

SAUCE Recipes

CIDER SAUCE

- **2 tablespoons butter**
- **⅓ cup flour**
- **1¾ cups ham broth or water**
- **½ cup cider**
- **½ cup apple jelly**

1. Melt butter; add flour; blend.
2. Add ham broth or water; stir; bring to boil.
3. Add cider, jelly; bring to boil.
4. Yield: approximately 2 cups sauce.
5. Serve with ham.

ORANGE SAUCE

- **3 tablespoons butter**
- **4 tablespoons flour**
- **1⅓ cups meat stock**
- **Salt**
- **Paprika**
- **1 tablespoon grated orange rind**
- **⅔ cup hot orange juice**
- **2 tablespoons sherry**

1. Melt butter; add flour; stir until slightly browned.
2. Add stock, salt, paprika; cook over boiling water until thickened.
3. Just before serving add orange rind, orange juice, sherry.
4. Yield: 2 cups sauce.
5. Serve with duck.

BLACK BUTTER SAUCE

- **2 tablespoons butter**
- **1 tablespoon lemon juice**
- **1 teaspoon minced parsley or capers**
- **⅛ teaspoon salt**
- **Pinch of pepper**
- **Pinch of paprika**

1. Heat butter in fry pan until lightly browned.
2. Add remaining ingredients; stir.
3. Yield: 3 tablespoons sauce.
4. Serve over steaks, chops.

QUICK MUSHROOM SAUCE

- **⅓ cup sliced onion**
- **2 tablespoons butter**
- **1 can condensed cream of mushroom soup**
- **1 cup milk**
- **¼ teaspoon salt**

1. Sauté onion in sauce pan in butter until tender and slightly browned.
2. Gradually stir in soup, milk; add salt.
3. Cook over low heat, stirring until bubbly.
4. Yield: approximately 2 cups sauce.
5. Serve with lamb chops.

Distinctively Styled

Meat Knives

Styled to complement the finest china and silver in your dining room and to be equally at home in your kitchen or at the barbecue grille.

Cutco's precision ground **Double D** blade retains a sharp edge longer — this, combined with the **Good Design** award-winning Lamb handle, forms an unbeatable combination.

OUTDOOR COOKERY

Building The Fire

The conventional way is to start with crumpled newspaper, topped with kindling wood as the bed for the charcoal. While this sounds simple, it does have disadvantages. One must chop the wood and it takes better than an hour to get the coals ready for cooking. The easiest way is to spray the charcoal with any one of several good fire starters to be found on the market, following the instructions on the container. Only a sheet of newspaper is needed for igniting and the coals are ready in ten to fifteen minutes. As a rule, less charcoal is needed because a single layer is sufficient for most charcoal broiling.

When the coals have all turned white on top and you can see a steady red glow underneath, the fire is ready. For best results, don't rush this preparation time. Flames, even little ones, do nothing but scorch the meat, spoiling the true charcoal flavor. It's better to be hungry a little longer than to serve meat resembling a piece of charred wood.

OUTDOOR Cookery

Alcoa Wrap A Must

Heavy Duty Alcoa Wrap is practically indispensable in Outdoor Cookery.

A sheet of foil accordion pleated into one inch pleats, placed under the charcoal, reflects the heat. The charcoal can be placed about an inch apart – thus less charcoal is needed.

When doing meat on the rotisserie, make the drip pan from Heavy Duty Alcoa Wrap. It catches all the fat and can be tossed away later.

For greater heat reflectivity, line sides and top of Barbecue with Heavy Duty Alcoa Wrap; also makes cleaning easier.

Shape double thick squares of Heavy Duty Alcoa Wrap into little bowls for holding sauces or garlic butter brushed onto meat during cooking. No pans to wash later.

Corn on the cob and potatoes, snugly wrapped in foil, may be cooked right in the coals; turn several times. Fresh or frozen vegetables, wrapped in Heavy Duty Alcoa Wrap can be done on the grill; turn packages several times to insure even cooking.

When cooking for a crowd and the grill is not large enough to cook all the meat at one time, keep the cooked batches hot by wrapping them in foil.

Use Heavy Duty Alcoa Wrap to keep corn on the cob and rolls hot during serving. Covering serving platters with foil eliminates dishwashing later.

Accessories

While you will find the Barbecue Shop in any store well stocked with all kinds of tricky gadgets, there are only a few that are really essential. It's wise to start with these and then let your pocketbook and your continued interest in outdoor cookery be your guide on future purchases.

Gloves—A pair of heavy canvas work gloves are indispensable for handling the charcoal when starting the fire. Asbestos gloves are good to have for adjusting the spit, moving hot coals when additional charcoal needs to be added or for other hot jobs.

Tongs—These are essential for turning broiled foods, for lifting potatoes from the coals or corn-on-the-cob from the grill. Since they are not expensive, it's smart to have at least two pairs.

OUTDOOR Cookery

Sprinkling Bottle—A large bottle with a sprinkler such as is used for sprinkling clothes is needed to extinguish flames that flare up during broiling. A tablespoon and a glass of water can serve the same purpose, but the sprinkler is more convenient.

Sauce Brush—A regular pastry brush with a fairly long handle is necessary for brushing meats either when broiling or doing meat on the spit. They are much easier to clean than a regular paint brush which has a tendency to shed its bristles.

Thermometer—A regular meat thermometer goes a long way toward doing a perfect roast over the grill. Knowing the right internal temperature is the only sure way of knowing the roast is done to your liking. Without a meat thermometer, you can only guess when the meat is done. All too often it will look done on the

outside, but be very much underdone in the center. Experts also like a regular thermometer to hang on the spit so as to know the temperature at which the meat is cooking. Of the two, the meat thermometer is the more important.

Hinged Broilers—Several of these with medium to fine grids are convenient for broiling bacon, chicken livers, oysters, tidbits, shrimp, etc.

Skewers—These should be 12-18 inches long and preferably of a non-rusting metal. They are desirable for all kinds of skewered foods. A Shish Kebab type of meal is not only economical, but allows each person to "cook his own" just the way he likes it.

Wire Brush—A stiff wire brush, resembling a regular scrubbing brush in size and shape, makes the cleaning of the grill an easy task.

OUTDOOR Cookery

Charcoal Roasting Time Chart

Beef

Standing Rib

	Thermometer Reading	Approximate Time
Rare	140° F.	2–2½ hours
Medium	140°–150° F.	2½–3 hours
Well Done	160°–170° F.	3–4 hours

Rolled Rib: Allow about 25–35 minutes longer. Thermometer reading will be the same.

Lamb

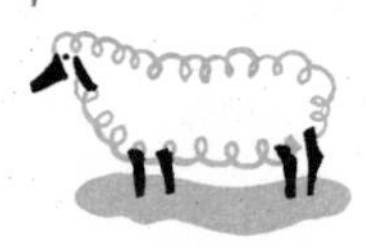

Leg

	Thermometer Reading	Approximate Time
Medium	150°–160° F.	1½–2 hours
Well Done	175°–180° F.	2–2½ hours

Boned Shoulder: Same as for Leg of Lamb.

Pork

	Thermometer Reading	Approximate Time
Fresh Loin	170°–175° F.	2–2½ hours
Fresh Ham—12 lb.	170°–175° F.	4 hours

OUTDOOR Cookery

Veal

	Thermometer Reading	Approximate Time
Rolled Roast—3-lb.	165°–170° F.	45–60 minutes

Poultry

	Approximate Time
Chicken—3–4 lbs.	1–1½ hours
Turkey—15 lbs.	3–4 hours
Duck—4–6 lbs.	1–1½ hours
Goose—4–7 lbs.	1¾–2½ hours
Rabbit—3–5 lbs.	40 minutes–2 hours
Wild Duck—1–2½ lbs.	20–30 minutes
Cornish Hens—1–2 lbs.	1–1½ hours

Charcoal Broiling Time Chart

Beef

Steaks

Thickness	Very Rare	Rare	Medium	Well Done
1 inch	6– 8 min.	8–12 min.	12–15 min.	15–20 min.
1½ inches	8–12 min.	10–15 min.	14–18 min.	18–25 min.
2 inches	14–20 min.	18–30 min.	25–30 min.	45–60 min.
2½ inches	20–30 min.	30–35 min.	35–45 min.	60–75 min.

Hamburgers

Rare	Medium	Well Done
10–12 min.	14–15 min.	18–20 min.

OUTDOOR Cookery

Lamb

Chops and Steaks

Thickness	Med. Rare	Well Done
1 inch	6–14 min.	18–25 min.
1½ inches	8–16 min.	20–30 min.
2 inches	12–20 min.	25–30 min.

Pork

Chops and Steaks

Pork should always be cooked slowly until well done but not dry.

Thickness	Time
1 inch	25–35 min.
1½ inches	30–45 min.

Ham Steaks

Thickness.	Time
¾ inch	25–30 min.
1 inch	30–35 min.
1½ inches	35–45 min.
2 inches	45–60 min.

OUTDOOR Cookery

Poultry

	Time
Chicken—split	25–45 min.
Duck—split	30–50 min.
Squab—split	25–35 min.

Fish

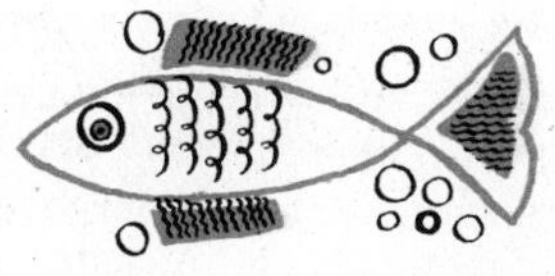

Fish Steaks

Thickness	Time
1 inch	6– 9 min.
1½ inches	8–12 min.
2 inches	10–18 min.

Fish Fillets

6–18 minutes depending on thickness.

Split Fish—small

8–12 minutes

Whole Fish—small

12–18 minutes

Whole Fish—large

30–60 minutes or until flesh flakes.

OUTDOOR Cookery

SHISH KEBAB

¾ cup oil
½ cup sauterne wine
1 tablespoon lemon juice
1 clove garlic, chopped
1 teaspoon salt
½ teaspoon pepper
3 pounds lean lamb, cut into 1½ inch cubes
12 small, egg-shaped tomatoes
6 small onions, cut in half
1 4-ounce can button mushrooms

1. Combine oil, wine, lemon juice, garlic, salt, pepper; blend well.
2. Place lamb cubes in large bowl; cover with marinade mixture.
3. Marinate in refrigerator overnight; remove 1 hour before serving time; drain; save marinade.
4. Alternate meat, tomatoes, onion halves, mushrooms on each of 6 long skewers.
5. Broil over hot coals, turning and basting with marinade frequently.
6. Allow 20 minutes for medium; 25 minutes for well done meat.
7. Yield: Six servings.

SHRIMP KEBAB

1 pound green shrimp, washed, cleaned
1 1-pound can pineapple chunks
¼ cup soy sauce
4 slices bacon, cut into 2-inch pieces

1. Place shrimp, pineapple chunks in bowl; top with soy sauce; let stand 30 minutes.
2. Alternate shrimp, pineapple, bacon pieces on small skewers.
3. Place each filled skewer in center of lightly greased square of Alcoa Wrap; bring up two sides of foil; fold over top of skewer, using double fold. Fold each end over twice, being careful not to pierce foil on tips of skewers.
4. Place foil packages on grill; broil, turning once.
5. Allow 12–14 minutes to thoroughly cook shrimp, bacon.
6. Serve each skewer in opened foil package.
7. Yield: Six to ten servings, depending on size of shrimp.

Note: These kebabs are delicious served as appetizers while broiling steaks, chops.

BARBECUED BROILERS

- 2 2-pound ready-to-cook broilers, halved
- 2 teaspoons lime juice
- ¼ cup oil
- 2 tablespoons vinegar
- 1 tablespoon Worcestershire sauce
- ⅛ teaspoon Tabasco sauce
- 1 teaspoon salt
- 1 teaspoon sugar
- ½ teaspoon garlic salt
- ½ teaspoon paprika

1. Clean, dry broilers; place in shallow pan.
2. Combine lime juice, oil, vinegar, Worcestershire sauce, Tabasco sauce, salt, sugar, garlic salt, paprika; blend well; pour over chicken.
3. Marinate 2 hours, turning once; remove; drain, saving marinade.
4. Place chicken on grill over medium coals, skin side up.
5. Broil until well done, turning and basting with marinade frequently.
6. Allow 35–40 minutes for well done chicken.
7. Yield: Four servings.

CHICKEN TEXAS

- 2 2-pound ready-to-cook broilers, halved
- 2 chicken bouillon cubes
- 1 cup boiling water
- ¼ cup oil
- 2 tablespoons ketchup
- 1 tablespoon Worcestershire sauce
- 1 teaspoon prepared horseradish
- 1 teaspoon sugar
- 1 teaspoon salt
- ½ teaspoon chili powder
- ½ teaspoon cayenne pepper
- 1 clove garlic, minced
- 1 small onion, chopped

1. Clean, dry broilers.
2. Dissolve bouillon cubes in boiling water.
3. Add oil, ketchup, Worcestershire sauce, horseradish, sugar, salt, chili powder, cayenne pepper, garlic, onion; blend well.
4. Pour into sauce pan; bring to a boil; cook 10 minutes over low heat.
5. Brush chicken with sauce; place on greased grill, skin side up.
6. Broil until well done, turning and basting with sauce frequently.
7. Allow 35–40 minutes for well done chicken.
8. Yield: Four servings.

CRUNCHY SHORT RIBS

- 3 pounds beef short ribs
- ¾ cup water
- ½ cup Worcestershire sauce
- 2 tablespoons lemon juice
- 2 tablespoons oil
- ¼ teaspoon Tabasco sauce
- ½ teaspoon garlic salt
- ¼ teaspoon pepper

1. Wipe meat with damp cloth; place in large bowl.
2. Combine water, Worcestershire sauce, lemon juice, oil, Tabasco sauce, garlic salt, pepper; blend well; pour over meat.
3. Marinate overnight in refrigerator, turning once.
4. Remove one hour before serving time; drain when ready to broil, saving marinade.
5. Broil over medium coals, turning and basting with marinade frequently.
6. Allow 35–45 minutes for well done meat.
7. Yield: Four servings.

GRILLED LAMB STEAKS

- 4 lamb steaks cut from leg, 1-inch thick
- ¾ cup olive oil
- ¼ cup vinegar
- 1 clove garlic, crushed
- 1 teaspoon salt
- ¼ teaspoon pepper
- ¼ teaspoon chopped fresh mint or ½ teaspoon crushed dried mint

1. Wipe meat with damp cloth; place in shallow baking pan.
2. Combine oil, vinegar, garlic, salt, pepper, mint; blend well; pour over meat.
3. Marinate in refrigerator 3–4 hours, turning once.
4. Remove when ready to broil; drain, saving marinade.
5. Grease grill well before placing steaks.
6. Broil, turning and basting with marinade frequently.
7. Allow 20–22 minutes for medium to well done steaks.
8. Yield: Four servings.

OUTDOOR Cookery

BARBECUED ROUND STEAK

1½ cups oil
½ cup vinegar
4 pounds top round steak, 1-inch thick
6 tablespoons ketchup
6 tablespoons Worcestershire sauce
1 teaspoon Tabasco sauce
2 teaspoons sugar
2 teaspoons salt
½ teaspoon pepper

1. Combine oil, vinegar.
2. Place steak in large bowl or baking pan.
3. Pour oil, vinegar mixture over steak; marinate overnight in refrigerator, turning several times.
4. Remove one hour before serving time; drain when ready to broil, saving marinade.
5. Combine ketchup, Worcestershire sauce, Tabasco sauce, sugar, salt, pepper; add ¾ cup marinade; heat.
6. Place steak on greased grill over coals.
7. Broil until done to taste, basting twice with the hot sauce.
8. Allow 8 minutes each side for rare; 10 minutes each side for medium; 12–14 minutes each side for well done.
9. Cut into serving pieces; serve with hot sauce.
10. Yield: Six servings.

BARBECUED SPARERIBS

4 pounds spareribs, cut into serving pieces
2 tablespoons salt
½ cup melted butter or margarine
½ cup chili sauce
2 tablespoons vinegar
1 tablespoon Worcestershire sauce
½ teaspoon garlic salt
½ teaspoon chili powder
¼ teaspoon pepper

1. Rub meat with salt.
2. Place in shallow roasting pan.
3. Bake 1 hour in moderate oven 350° F.; baste 3 or 4 times with meat drippings.
4. In sauce pan, combine melted butter, chili sauce, vinegar, Worcestershire sauce, garlic salt, chili powder, pepper; blend well; cook 10 minutes over low heat.
5. Remove meat from oven; place on grill; broil, basting with sauce frequently. Turn only once.
6. Allow 30 minutes for well done meat.
7. Yield: Four servings.

SKEWERED LIVER AND BACON

- 2 pounds calves liver, cut 1½ inches thick
- 12 slices bacon
- 12 mushroom caps
- 2 tablespoons oil

1. Wipe liver with damp cloth; cut into 12 1½ inch cubes.
2. Place liver, bacon, mushroom caps on skewers, alternating in order given; put 2 pieces of each on a skewer.
3. Brush each piece with oil.
4. Place skewers on grill; broil until bacon is crisp.
5. Allow 10–12 minutes broiling time.
6. Yield: Six servings.

BARBECUED HAM STEAKS

- 2 uncooked smoked ham steaks, 1-inch thick
- 1 cup cider
- 3 tablespoons brown sugar
- 1 tablespoon dry mustard
- 3 whole cloves, crushed

1. Trim excess fat from ham; score edges at 1-inch intervals.
2. Place in large fry pan; cover with boiling water; parboil 5 minutes.
3. Pour water off steaks.
4. Combine cider, brown sugar, mustard, cloves; blend well.
5. Pour over steaks; marinate 15 minutes; drain, saving marinade.
6. Grease grill with fat trimmings.
7. Broil over medium coals until brown on both sides, turning and basting with marinade frequently.
8. Allow 30-35 minutes for well done, browned meat.
9. Yield: Four to Six servings.

PIZZA FILLED FRANKS

- 6 frankfurters
- 2 tablespoons grated Parmesan cheese
- 2 tablespoons grated American cheese
- 1 small tomato, chopped fine
- ¼ teaspoon garlic salt
- ¼ teaspoon oregano
- ⅛ teaspoon pepper
- 6 strips bacon

1. Score frankfurters in half lengthwise, being careful not to cut all the way through.
2. Combine Parmesan cheese, American cheese, tomato, garlic salt, oregano, pepper; blend well.
3. Fill frankfurters with mixture.
4. Wrap bacon strips around filled frankfurters, spiral fashion; secure with toothpicks.
5. Place frankfurters crosswise over grill wires.
6. Broil over hot coals, turning frequently, until bacon is done.
7. Allow 7-9 minutes broiling time.
8. Yield: Six servings.

OUTDOOR Cookery

Go Withs

While the entrée done over charcoal is the focal point of most outdoor eating, other foods are essential or desirable for a well balanced meal. These should be simple and in keeping with the informality of the occasion. Avoid anything that requires last minute preparation or that cannot be kept waiting if necessary. Here are a few suggestions:

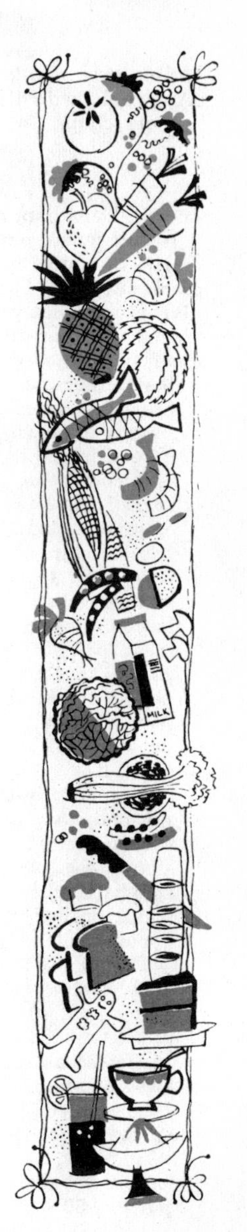

Appetizers

Tomato Juice—Vegetable Juice—Pineapple Juice—Apricot Nectar.

Relish Tray of Pickles—Olives—Celery—Green Onions—Carrot Sticks—Green Pepper Strips.

Shrimp with Hot Sauce—Chopped Chicken Livers—Herring in Sour Cream—Melon Balls or Wedges with Lemon.

Vegetables

Potatoes wrapped in Alcoa Wrap baked in the coals—Corn-on-the-Cob wrapped in aluminum foil done on back of grill—Escalloped or Au Gratin Potatoes—Hash Brown Potatoes—Potato Salad—Baked Beans—Corn Pudding—Green Beans and Mushrooms—Harvard Beets—Braised Celery—Hubbard Squash.

Salads

Tossed Green Salad—Cole Slaw—Cucumber and Onion with Sour Cream Dressing—Tomato and Onion—Molded Vegetable—Italian Salad—Green Bean Salad.

Breads

Crisp crusted Rye or Pumpernickel—Garlic Bread—French or Italian Bread—Corn Sticks—Hard Rolls—Butter Crust Rolls.

Desserts

Fresh Fruit with Cookies—Cake—Pie—Ice Cream—Ice Cream and Cake Roll—Fruit Tarts—Grapefruit—Melon.

Beverages

Hot Tea—Hot Coffee—Iced Tea or Coffee—Milk—Lemonade—Soft Drinks—Soda Pop.

Index

D

E

F

G

H

Index

R

S

Index

Courtesy American Meat Institute